LOOK
BEFORE YOU
LEASE
SECRETS TO SMART
VEHICLE LEASING

by
Michael Scott Kranitz, Esq.

Buy-Rite Holdings, Incorporated, Concord, Massachusetts

LOOK BEFORE YOU LEASE: SECRETS TO SMART VEHICLE LEASING. Copyright ©1997 by Michael Scott Kranitz. All rights reserved. Printed in the United States of America. No part of this book may be reproduced or transmitted in any form or by any means, electronic or mechanical, including photocopying, recording, or by any information storage and retrieval system, without prior written permission from the publisher.

Trademarks
In certain places in this book, trademarked names are used. Our use of these names is intended solely for the benefit of the trademark owner, with no intention of infringement of the trademark. Where those designations appear in this book, the designations have been printed with initial capitalization and appropriate trademark notations.

Gender Usage
Use of the masculine gender throughout this book is for ease of reading and convenience only. This text is intended to be gender neutral.

Library of Congress Catalog Card Number: 96-80463
ISBN: 1-889093-04-1

Distributed by National Book Network

Cover design by Richard Chandler and SyWaldman

Additional copies of this book may be obtained by contacting the publisher at:

Buy-Rite Holdings, Incorporated
Damonmill Square
Suite 5A4
Concord, Massachusetts 01742
Phone: (508) 371-0015
Fax: (508) 371-1487

Dedicated to my father Marc Kranitz who, after 20 years of leasing cars, has never been offered a deal he could not improve.

Contents

APPENDICES

Introduction

In 1997, leasing is expected to account for roughly 40% of all new and used vehicle acquisitions. And, with the price of cars steadily rising, more and more consumers will turn to leasing as their preferred method of financing. Yet, despite its popularity, surprisingly few consumers actually understand how leasing really works. According to the Consumer Federation of America, complaints about auto leasing doubled in 1996. The chief complaint among consumers was their inability to understand the lease contract. Simply put, leasing is more complex than buying. No matter how adept you might be at negotiating, determining whether you have maximized your potential on any given deal is nearly impossible if you do not have a good working knowledge of the mechanics of leasing. Don't rely on the dealer to tell you that you "really got him" on your deal. Make that judgment yourself.

This book can enable you to do just that. In about an hour or so, you should be able to digest the concepts in this book well enough to save yourself hundreds and possibly thousands of dollars on your next vehicle lease! Even savvy consumers will appreciate the insights, practical hints and explanation of the recently approved Federal disclosure regulations.

Throughout this book, you will encounter highlighted terms which are defined in Chapter Twelve—*The Language of Leasing*. As you read, you may find it useful to refer ahead to that chapter to enhance your understanding of the concepts discussed. Although not necessary, a pencil and calculator may also be helpful as you work through some of the examples. After you've gone through a few calculations, you can test your skills on any of the myriad lease advertisements in your magazines or newspapers. Once you've tackled a few of those, you should be able to stride into any dealership with confidence that the process of leasing will be both an enjoyable and rewarding one.

The Idea Behind Leasing

The first thing you should know when leasing a vehicle is that someone is actually *buying* the vehicle—it's just not you. In most lease deals, the **lessor** (usually a bank, independent leasing company or captive finance company such as GMAC, Toyota Motor Credit, etc.) buys the vehicle from the dealer or manufacturer and then leases it to you. You, in turn, pay the lessor for the right to drive the vehicle during the **term** of your lease.

An Overview

The monthly payments made on a vehicle lease are quite different from monthly payments on a vehicle loan. Unlike a loan payment, which is made up of principal and interest components, a lease payment is an amalgamation of depreciation, lease charges, insurance charges, miscellaneous fees and, in most states, prorated taxes. The largest portion of any lease payment typically goes to compensate the lessor for the vehicle's decline in value, or **depreciation,** over the lease term. The second largest component is called the **lease charge** or **lease rate.** This, the cost of money, akin to interest in a loan balance. Remember, a lessor must buy the vehicle in order to lease it to you. Naturally, he will expect you to pay for the use of his funds (plus a profit) until you return the vehicle. The lease rate provides the lessor a return on his money (in some cases, the rate may include the cost of gap insurance—discussed later). Finally, your monthly payment includes a fraction of the any front-end fees or charges tacked onto the vehicle's cost, such as after-market product charges (i.e. extended warranties) and an **acquisition fee.**

At the end of your lease, you may do one of four things:

- Return the vehicle to its rightful owner (the lessor). This is called a "walkaway" in the industry;

 - Trade your leased vehicle in on a new one. If there is "equity" in the vehicle (in other words, the vehicle is worth more than what you would have to pay the leasing company to buy it), it won't cost you anything other than, perhaps, a **disposition fee** to trade it in on a new vehicle. This will typically not be the case until you are near the end of your lease (in some cases, you may never have equity);

- Purchase the vehicle outright from the lessor, usually for an amount equal to the **residual value** stated in your lease agreement plus additional fees (most lessors tack on a profit of 5–25% of the residual value); or

- Extend the lease for some limited period, usually at the same monthly rate.

7

Usually, returning the vehicle is your best option. As you will see when we do the numbers, once you have completed your lease payments, digging farther into your pocket to pay (or finance) the typically inflated purchase option price is like buying the vehicle more than once. If, when making your deal, you think you might wish to keep the vehicle beyond the original term of the lease, you are probably better off buying it rather than leasing it.

If you terminate your lease early, expect to pay dearly for the privilege. Most leases require you to pay the remaining amounts due under the lease as well as a termination penalty which is intended to cover the lessor's lost profit and cost of disposing of your vehicle. Early termination is usually such an undesirable option that you will be motivated to stay in the lease until the end of its term. The costs of early termination are explored more fully in Chapter Eight: *Termination—A Clause for Concern.*

Leasing Versus Buying—A Quick Look

In order to more fully appreciate the characteristics of a lease, it is helpful to compare and contrast them with the attributes of a normally financed vehicle. Here are some of the major features of both:

- You do not own a leased vehicle. You do own a financed vehicle though the lender holds a lien on it.

- You may not permanently modify a leased vehicle unless permitted by the lessor (usually at a great cost to you).

- You are responsible for repairs and maintenance on a leased vehicle just as if you had purchased it. (Although more and more manufacturers, such as BMW, are offering regularly scheduled maintenance with certain leases).

- With a leased vehicle, <u>you must pay for miles</u> driven in excess of the amount permitted under the lease.

 You are liable to the lessor for all damage to a leased vehicle other than ordinary wear and tear (a term which is typically left vague by the lessor).

- You can often lease a vehicle for no down payment. Typically, lenders require a 10–20% down payment on a purchased vehicle.

- When you purchase a vehicle, you bear all of the risk and cost of the vehicle's decline in value. In a closed-end lease, the lessor bears this risk and you have the luxury of deciding at the end of the lease whether to purchase it and, in some cases, at what price.

A Peek Behind The Monthly Payment

Of primary importance to most consumers is size of their monthly payment. In virtually all cases, a monthly lease payment will be smaller than a monthly loan payment on the same vehicle. To intelligently compare the two, you must understand the different ways in which monthly lease and monthly loan payments are calculated. With a vehicle loan, your payments are based solely on the purchase price of the vehicle. In other words, you pay equal monthly payments which, over the life of the loan, go to repay the purchase price plus interest. With an amortization table or a calculator, it is fairly easy to figure your approximate monthly payments on a vehicle loan.

On the other hand, calculating a lease and comparing lease deals is a bit more complicated. Although not extremely difficult, determining a lease payment has been made difficult for most consumers because dealers and leasing companies in most states have not, to date, been legally required to volunteer elements essential to determining the lease payment, such as the capitalized cost and lease rate or money factor. Trying to calculate a lease payment without these numbers is like trying to figure a mortgage without knowing the principal amount of your loan or the interest rate being charged! Although the federal government, individual states and even leasing companies have taken steps to have this and additional information clearly disclosed, the business of calculating and comparing lease deals is inherently more complex than calculating a simple loan payment and comparing it to another. Even if furnished with the necessary information, relatively few consumers know how to generate an accurate lease payment. Yet, day after day, and in ever-increasing numbers, consumers continue to blindly sign leases, never knowing whether they are paying too much for their vehicles. Understanding why is easy. On the same vehicle, lease payments usually appear so much more attractive than loan payments that consumers often believe they are getting a wonderful deal right off the bat and press only enough to get minor reductions in their monthly payments. Unfortunately, a deal that seems favorable at first glance usually has substantial

12

room for improvement, and the only way to truly know whether your lease deal is a good one is to understand it thoroughly.

The next few chapters take you, step-by-step, through the calculation of a lease payment. Once you learn the method, you will instantly elevate yourself into the small percentage of people who can analyze and knowledgeably negotiate their lease deal.

A Lease's Pieces

2

E ven if you hate math, you owe it to yourself to become intimately familiar with the method of calculating and analyzing monthly lease payments. The ability to understand and manipulate the numbers that make up your lease quote will be the most powerful tool in your bargaining arsenal. After all, you will never know if you have truly obtained the best deal possible if you know nothing about how the dealer arrived at the monthly payment he quoted. In this arena, knowledge is cash. If you just refuse to get down and dirty with numbers directly, a software program like *LeaseWizard*™ can do the calculations for you and recommend ways to improve your deal (See Appendix A). Whichever method you choose, you should become acquainted with the four basic components of all vehicle lease payments.

The Four Basics of a Lease Payment

In order to analyze any lease payment, you must know the following four elements:

- Adjusted Capitalized Cost
- Residual Value
- Lease Rate
- Lease Term

Once you have these items, you can crank through your quote and determine whether the offer proposed by your dealer is satisfactory to you and whether the dealer gave you all of the terms you thought you had bargained for during your visit. Let's explore each element in detail.

Adjusted Capitalized Cost

The beginning point in the calculation of any lease payment is the **capitalized cost** (or cap cost). The cap cost is equivalent to the negotiated "purchase price" of the vehicle. If you have negotiated even the least bit, your cap cost should be less than the Manufacturer's Suggested Retail Price (the **MSRP** or "sticker" price). The cap cost also includes any after-market option charges and fees which you agree to roll into your lease payment, such as **acquisition fees, dealer preparation** or **destination fees**[1], and document fees, if any. The cap cost will be reduced by the amount of any **down payment, trade in allowance** or **dealer discount.** These adjustments are called **cap cost reductions.** After all adjustments are made, the final cap cost is referred to as the **adjusted cap cost.** The adjusted cap cost is analogous to a final purchase price.

Residual Value

The residual value of a leased vehicle is the lessor's estimate of what the vehicle will be worth at the end of your lease term. Sometimes referred to as

---

[1]Some states prohibit dealers from passing dealer preparation or dealer destination charges on to customers if they (the dealers) expect to be reimbursed by the manufacturer for these costs.

the "lease-end value," the residual value is an important number to know because your payments will be based on the difference between the adjusted capitalized cost and the residual value of the vehicle (we will discuss this fully in Chapter Three— *Assembling the Pieces*). Residual values are figured as a percentage of the vehicle's MSRP. For example, a $25,000 MSRP and a 50% residual factor will result in an estimated $12,500 residual value at lease end. You can get a pretty good idea of what the industry thinks the residual value of your vehicle should be by consulting publications such as the *Automotive Lease Guide* or the *Kelley Blue Book*. See Appendix A to learn how to obtain these guides).

Residual values will vary depending upon the particular model you choose, the lessor (i.e. bank, captive finance company or independent leasing company), the amount of miles you anticipate driving, and particular promotions being offered on that model. In virtually all cases, the lessor—not the dealer—sets the residual value and the best you can do is shop among different lessors for the most competitive number. Sometimes it pays to consider an entirely different make or model if, for example, one auto maker is offering an extremely aggressive value.[2] Usually, you will shop for the highest residual value possible because **the higher the residual value, the lower your monthly payment will be,** all other things being equal. This occurs because the residual value is subtracted from the adjusted cap cost to arrive at the amount you must repay over the lease term.

Believe it or not, there are times when you might **not** wish to have a high residual value. If you are planning to enter into an open-end lease, for example, you may be safer with a less aggressive residual value. In an open-end lease, you are liable for the difference between the predicted residual value and the actual amount received by the lessor on the sale or auction of your vehicle at lease end. If your residual value was artificially inflated to reduce your

---

[2]In the summer of 1996, Acura was offering a **75%** residual value on certain CL models in order to introduce them to the public.

monthly payments, you will end up paying the price at lease end if the true value of the vehicle is lower. If you are seriously considering a lease-end purchase, you may also be a candidate for a lower residual value because that amount will be the **minimum** you will be expected to pay for the vehicle (many lessors charge 105–125% of the residual value). Of course, you must balance that possible savings against higher monthly payments. A low residual value also makes good sense if you are leasing a vehicle for business purposes and you have the opportunity to purchase it for personal use at lease end. Provided the vehicle is actually being used for business, the higher monthly payments may be deducted as a business expense during the course of the lease, leaving a reasonable purchase option amount for you at lease end.[3] Finally, if you believe you may wish to terminate your lease early for any reason, too high a residual value is undesirable because it will result in a higher

---

[3] Discuss the deductibility of your lease payment with your accountant before entering into a lease for a tax advantage.

termination penalty (See Chapter Eight: *Termination: A Clause For Concern* for a full discussion).

Unless you fit into one of those categories, however, you will likely find yourself shopping for a high residual value in order to obtain a lower monthly payment. Manufacturers are aware of this and often "push" the residual value in order to advertise and deliver lower monthly payments. This usually operates to your benefit. Keep in mind, however, that the residual value may be a double-edged sword in an open-end lease or if you intend to either purchase your vehicle or terminate your lease early.

TIP: Keep an eye out for residual values that look too high to be true. They may be coupled with higher-than-market lease rates. The key is to shop **all** elements of your lease.

Lease Rate

For reasons not apparent to ordinary folks, the term "interest" is absent from most lease documents and, seemingly, from the vocabularies of most people in the vehicle leasing business as well. Instead, you will find terms such as **lease rate, lease charge, lease factor** or **money factor.** In their purest form, these charges all reflect the same thing—the "cost of money!"

Lease rates and money factors are "rates" but they appear nothing like ordinary interest rates which are expressed in annual percentages. Nonetheless, with minimal manipulation, you can convert a lease rate or money factor into a number which closely approximates an annual interest rate comparable to loan rates offered in the marketplace. A lease **charge,** on the other hand, is not a rate. It is an actual dollar amount expressed either as a monthly charge or a total charge over the life of the lease. These charges can be converted into lease rates or money factors which, in turn, may be converted into approximate annual interest rates. But, before you fire up your calculator for lease rate conversion, understand that a lease rate (or money factor) is not equivalent to a simple APR (annual percentage rate) charged in a loan. Although we can approximate an annual interest rate with a given lease rate, unless you run a full-blown internal rate of return analysis, you're unlikely to stumble upon the exact APR rate being charged under your lease. Fortunately, automobile leasing is not nuclear physics where infinitely precise numbers are always needed. For the vast majority of consumers, a close approximation will do fine for comparing deals. Nonetheless, before we leap into the lease rate arena, it is useful to explore the problems surrounding lease rates and what to watch out for when reading advertisements boasting low "interest rates" on leases.

Wrestling With the Rate

You may be surprised to learn that a lease rate is usually comprised of more than just a rate of return on the lessor's money. Other costs in addition to the cost of money go into the lease rate. These items range from profit on the rate of "interest" being charged to gap insurance premiums or fees associated with the purchase of the vehicle at lease end. Since different lessors calculate their lease rates differently, there is no way for consumers to precisely compare rates-to-rates among dealers unless they know what goes into each dealer's lease rate. Even a lease rate without built-in charges will not reflect the annual percentage rate being charged, as we have come to know that term in the finance world. Although the detailed reasons for this are beyond the scope of this book, suffice it to say that the infinitely different ways a lease can be constructed make it nearly impossible to provide a simple method for consumers to determine the effective APR under any given lease. In fact, the federal government, consumer groups, finance experts and individual state governments have yet to agree on exactly what an advertised lease rate should reflect or how to express it in a uniform way that makes it easy for consumers to compare different deals on an apples-to-apples basis. For that reason (along with others explored in Chapter 9—*Leasing Legislation*), the new regulations under the Consumer Leasing Act will not require lease rate disclosure.

Thanks for the Education—What Now?

So does this mean you must close your eyes and ignore the lease rate until government agencies and industry leaders can agree on a workable solution? **No way!** You should begin by asking your dealer for the money factor, lease factor or level yield factor. They are all the same thing—a number which reflects, for the most part, the cost of money which the lessor is charging you over the term of your lease. If the dealer refuses or explains that interest is not really charged under the lease, show him what you look like walking out of the dealership no matter how far along you are in the process. There is a money factor being applied and it can be roughly translated into an annual interest rate for your analysis. If asked, most dealers will furnish you with that information. At the very least, the dealer should be able to give you the monthly or annual lease charges from which you can derive approximate rates. So, let's see how to do it!

Money Factor and Annual Interest Rate

The money factor is a puny looking number which, when multiplied by the sum of the adjusted

25

cap cost and the residual value, gives the lessor (and you) the monthly "interest" component of your lease payment. Usually, the number will be a fraction with at least two 0's followed by two or three more digits (i.e. .0035 or .00312).[4] Of course, this enigmatic little fraction is of little use to you (and could possibly be misleading) if you cannot put it into a meaningful context. To convert the money factor into a close approximation of the annual interest rate being charged under your lease you should first determine whether the number you have been given is a money factor or what purports to be a percentage rate. For example, if you were told "two-nine" you might not know whether the rate being charged was 2.9% or a .0029 money factor (which is approximately equal to

---

[4]Sometimes, the money factor is expressed as a fraction 1000 times smaller than the "typical" money factor (i.e. .0000035). While that type can easily be converted by moving the decimal point a few places, some companies, like Ford Motor Credit have money factors that do not even remotely look like those used by the majority of players in the industry. Check Appendix D for a method to convert their latest money factor formula into one you can deal with reasonably.

6.9%). The two are quite different. For this calculation, **make sure you have a money factor!** Next, you should ask what charges other than the cost of money (if any) have been figured into the money factor, such as gap premiums, option fees, etc. . . . If there are other charges, find out what was added so you know when comparing it to other money factors. If there are other charges included in your money factor or lease rate, don't bother trying to parse them out to determine what the pure rate is without them. It's usually not worth your time and the result you get using the "gross" lease factor is just as useful for comparison purposes provided you know what has been added into the competing dealer's lease charges.

Power Up Your Calculator!

Assuming the dealer gives you a money factor of .0035 and you wish to know the approximate annual rate, first multiply the money factor by 2400 as shown.

Example 2:1

.0035 x 2400 = **8.4% Approximate Annual Rate**[5]

To further enhance the accuracy of your calculation, one lease finance expert recommends you subtract .10 (10 basis points) from the result for every year the lease term exceeds 12 months. In our example above, the approximate annual rate on a 36-month lease would be:

Example 2:2

8.4% − .20% = **8.20% Approximate Annual Rate**

---

[5]Actually, multiplying by **24** will give you .084, the correct representation of 8.4%. Using **2400**, however, dispenses with the need to move any decimals—just add a "%" and you have it!

Caution: Whatever you do, use the given money factor when calculating your payment. That is the number the dealer will use. The effective annual rate is for comparison purposes only!

On the other hand, if the dealer quotes you an annual rate, but uses a money factor in the calculations (likely), you can cross-check the quoted rate by simply reversing the equation and dividing the money factor by 2400 as shown.

Example 2:3

$$\frac{8.4\% \text{ Annual Rate}}{2400} = .0035 \textbf{ Money Factor}$$

Monthly or Total Lease Charges

Often, lessors and dealers will express the cost of money in terms of total or monthly **lease charges,** rather than as an annual interest rate or money factor. For example, the dealer may quote you total lease charges of **$5,750** on a 48-month lease. Like the money factor or lease rate, in order to fully use this information, you must first find out how much of the charge is made up of "interest charges" and how much is comprised of other fees and charges. If the charges can be broken out, you can obtain a good approximation of the annual interest rate equivalent (an implicit rate) by performing the following calculations.

First, subtract the "other charges" included in the total lease charge. Then convert the total lease charge into a monthly lease charge by dividing it by the term of the lease.

Example 2:4

a. $5,750   – $750   = $5,000
   Lease Charge – Other Charges = Total Rate

b. $\dfrac{\$5,000}{48 \text{ mos.}}$ = **$104.16/month in interest**

The resulting figure ($104.16 here) is the portion of your monthly payment, on average, that goes to pay for interest. Next, obtain the approximate equivalent money factor by dividing the $104.16 monthly interest charge by the sum of the adjusted cap cost and the residual value. In our example, if the adjusted cap cost is $18,000 and the residual value is $8,700, the money factor can be calculated as follows:

Example 2:5

$$\frac{\$104.16}{\$26,700} \quad \frac{\text{(monthly charge)}}{(\$18,000 + \$8,700)} \quad = \quad \begin{array}{l}\textbf{.0039} \\ \textbf{Money Factor}\end{array}$$
$$\text{Adj. Cap + Residual}$$

If you want to know the approximate annual rate, simply multiply the money factor by 2400 as described in the previous section and you get:

Example 2:6

.0039 x 2400 = **9.36% Annual Rate**[6]

---

[6]As illustrated in Example 2.2, for a more accurate estimate you can subtract .10 from the result for each year the term exceeds 12 months. Also, note that in this example we deducted fees and other charges before calculating the approximate annual rate, but did not do so in our previous Example 2.2.

Did you notice how a mere difference of **.0004** from the .0035 money factor in Example 2:2, and the .0039 money factor from Example 2:4 resulted in nearly a full percentage point increase in the approximate annual rate of interest?! Keep your eye on the money factor.

TIP: Keep in mind that the lease rate is only one measure of comparison among leases and you should not rely upon it exclusively when comparing two or more leases. Compare **all** aspects of your lease offers!

Lease Term

Although a longer lease term yields a lower monthly payment, be wary of lengthy leases. As a rule of thumb, the term of your lease should not exceed the life of the warranties covering your vehicle. If your budget forces you to consider only leases with terms exceeding the vehicle warranty, you are usually better off looking at a less expensive vehicle. Otherwise, you risk having to pay for major repairs to a vehicle you do not own. Another consideration when deciding on the term length is how long it will take before the actual resale value of the car exceeds the cost of terminating the lease early, allowing you to economically move into a different vehicle. Generally, you can expect to be "upside down" (in other words, you will owe more than the car is worth) on your lease until you have paid at least 75% of the payments due under the lease. The actual value of your vehicle, of course, will depend on a number of factors, including, model year, condition, mileage, and the demand for that particular vehicle type in your region.

Assembling The Pieces

3

N ow that you know the four essential pieces of the lease puzzle, let's see how they fit together. As we have seen, a monthly lease payment is based not on the purchase price of the vehicle, but rather, on the vehicle's estimated decline in value over the term of the lease. This decline in value is the vehicle's **depreciation** and it is measured by the difference between the **adjusted cap cost** of the vehicle (including up-front fees) and the vehicle's estimated **residual value** at the end of the lease. The total of your monthly payments equals the depreciation plus lease charges, fees and taxes. Over the life of your lease, most of your payments go toward payment of depreciation. Think of your monthly payments as compensation to the lessor for the decline in the value of his asset while you are using it. The lease charge, which represents the second largest component of your payment, is payment for use of the lessor's funds plus a profit.

Anatomy of a Monthly Payment

Let's examine a vehicle with an adjusted cap cost of $18,000 and an estimated residual value of $8,000. By subtracting the residual value from the adjusted cap cost, we know that this vehicle will experience $10,000 in estimated depreciation over the term of the lease. Accordingly, the monthly lease payments will go to repay the $10,000 in depreciation plus lease charges, fees and taxes. (By contrast, if the vehicle were financed, the monthly payments would go to repay the entire $18,000 plus interest, fees and taxes). The monthly lease payment has two major components: depreciation and the cost of money.

Depreciation Component

By simply dividing the total depreciation by the lease term, you can figure out the *depreciation component* of your monthly lease payment. In this case, $10,000 in depreciation over a three-year lease term results in a monthly depreciation component of $277 ($10,000 ÷ 36 months). On average, depreciation makes up the bulk of your monthly lease payment.[7]

Cost of Money Component

The second largest component of your lease payment is the cost of money (lease rate). Most of us are used to the concept of interest, especially as it relates to credit cards, car loans and mortgages. But unlike those forms of financing, where you pay interest on the balance you are repaying (i.e. the principal), a vehicle lease requires you to pay interest on both the principal amount being repaid (the depreciation), as *well* as the residual value, which you are not repaying. You pay interest on the residual value in order to compensate the lessor for your "use" of those funds during the term of your lease.

---

[7]Typically, the portion of your monthly payment being allocated to depreciation will increase over the life of the lease. This is also a characteristic of a typically amortized loan.

Remember, in order to lease the vehicle to you, the lessor had to purchase it first for a price which equaled the depreciation **plus** the residual value. In that sense, the lessor was no different from a bank which would have paid the dealer the entire purchase price of the vehicle and then charged you interest for the use of its funds. Whether leasing or financing a vehicle, you can be certain that you will pay for the use of someone else's money.

Dissecting A Deal

Armed with the fundamental concepts, you are now ready to dig into a full analysis. In the following exercise we will examine how much it will cost to lease a truck which retails for $19,350. We will assume the following facts:

1. ADJUSTED CAP COST—**$18,000**
   Having researched the pricing guides thoroughly, you succeed in negotiating the

price down to $18,000.[8] We will assume that you will not be making a down payment or trading in a vehicle and that the $18,000 is inclusive of all up-front charges.

2. **RESIDUAL VALUE—$8,000**
    Based on predicted usage and other factors, in four years the truck will be worth an estimated 41.3% of the MSRP, or $8,000.

3. **MONEY FACTOR—.00312**
    Lease rates on vehicle leases vary according to market interest rates and particular promotions offered by manufacturers. Usually, captive finance companies (i.e. those affiliated with the vehicle manufacturer) as well as large banks offer the most aggressive lease rates. In our example, we assume a money factor of .00312.

---

[8] In certain cases, such as with subvented leases, the dealer may not be able to use a bargain purchase price (with rebates, for example) as the initial capital cost in a lease deal.

For those of you who were paying attention, this translates into an approximate annual interest rate of 7.3%.[9]

4.   TERM—**36 Months**
Since you usually get the itch for a new truck every two or three years, the 36-month term seems to meet your needs.

Although there is more than one way to figure your lease payment with the four essential elements, the following is the simplest way to accurately chug through the numbers. Keep in mind, however, that this example does not include back-end fees or lease-end charges, which will not be included in your monthly payment.

---

[9].00312 x 24 = 7.488%. 7.488% – .20 (3-year lease rate adjustment) = 7.288%.

Example 3:1

1.   Calculate The Depreciation Component

A. Adj. Cap   Residual   Total
    Cost   – Value   =   Depreciation
    $18,000   – $8,000   =   10,000

B. Total   Lease   Monthly
    Depreciation ÷ Term   =   Depreciation
    $10,000   ÷ 36 mos.   = $277.77

The depreciation component is simply the amount by which the vehicle will decline in value over the lease term divided by the term, itself.

2.   Calculate The Cost of Money Component

A. Adj. Cap   Residual   Lease Balance
    Cost   + Value   =   Multiplier
    $18,000   + $8,000   = $26,000

B. Lease Balance   Money   **Monthly**
    Multiplier   x Factor =   **Lease Charge**
    $26,000   x .00312 =   **$ 81.12**

Since the lessor must purchase the entire vehicle, you will compensate the lessor on the entire cost of the car. This amount is calculated by multiplying the money

41

factor by the sum of the residual value and the adjusted cap cost.

3.   Total Monthly Lease Payment

Monthly Depreciation	+	Monthly Interest	=	**Monthly Payment**
$277.77	+	$81.12	=	**$358.89**

Adding the two components yields your monthly payment of $358.89, excluding fees and taxes.

The Sales Tax

It is almost unimaginable for a dealer to quote you his "best price" with sales tax included. It only raises the price and it's not his fault that you have to pay taxes. Unfortunately, it does not matter whose fault it is—you **will** pay sales tax on your leased vehicle so don't ignore it! Calculating the monthly payment including tax is actually simple in most states. For a full discussion of tax calculations and related issues, refer to Chapter 10—*Just the Tax.*

✝ Fee Advice

So where do the fees come in? Usually, the acquisition fee, destination charge, prep charge, and official fees are added directly to the cap cost and "rolled" into your lease payment, unless you pay for them in cash up front. In addition, the cost to "purchase" an increase in your annual mileage allowance will also find its way into the mix and trickle down to your monthly payment.[10] On the other hand, disposition fees and purchase option fees will be assessed by the lessor at lease end along with any penalties, damage charges or excess mileage charges.

Dividing The Pie

The following chart illustrates how the monthly lease payment is allocated, on average, for a $20,000 car with a monthly payment of $338.00 (including tax

---

[10]Since additional miles cause greater wear on your vehicle, the cost to purchase them is reflected in a lower residual value. The difference that makes in your monthly payment is often quantified in a per-mile charge for your convenience.

at 5.75%), and a 7.51% approximate annual rate of interest.

Where Does Your Lease Dollar Go?
Typical Allocation of $338 Payment

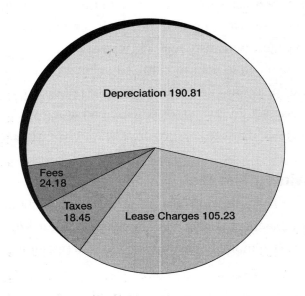

Depreciation 190.81

Fees 24.18

Taxes 18.45

Lease Charges 105.23

On most leases, the portion of your payment devoted to interest will decrease and the portion devoted to depreciation will increase as the term elapses.

Putting It In Perspective: Lease vs. Loan

4

To intelligently assess whether leasing is a better alternative for you than buying, you should compare the monthly payments, as well as additional financial and non-financial aspects of both forms of financing. Since monthly payments usually rank first among consumers' financial concerns, let's begin with them.

Getting More For Your Monthlies

Low monthly payments are easily the most attractive feature of a lease. Lease payments give consumers the ability to drive what they cannot otherwise afford. To illustrate the power of leasing, here is a comparison of the monthly payments for a vehicle with an MSRP of $25,000 and a negotiated purchase price of $22,500.

Table 4:1

	Lease	Loan
Purchase Price	$22,500	$22,500
Acquisition Fee/Origination Fee	$250	$250
Down Payment	<$500>	<$4,500>
Cap Cost/Amount Financed	**$22,250**	**$18,250**
Residual Value (after 36 mo. term)	<$12,000>	Not Applicable
Payments Will Be Based On...	**$10,250**	**$18,250**
Monthly Payment (9% Annual Rate)*	$436.92	$613.72

*Includes 5.75% sales tax included in each monthly payment

The monthly lease payment on this vehicle is about $177 lower than the monthly loan payment, even with a $4,500 down payment reducing the amount financed on the purchase side. Talk about leverage! Of course, one cannot ignore the fact that the purchaser's down payment will turn up at the end of the loan as owner's equity in the vehicle (which he will keep), whereas the lessee will have nothing to show for his payments at lease end. Nonetheless, from the example given above, it is easy to understand why monthly payments are the most powerful and attractive feature of a lease. In the following sections, we will explore the following monetary and non-monetary factors to consider when deciding whether to lease or buy:

- total cash outlay
- immediate cash outlay
- the desire to drive a more expensive vehicle
- how long you expect to drive the vehicle
- loss of cash used for a down payment

Lease vs. Loan vs. Cash

In this example, we are looking at a new car with an MSRP of $19,800, a final selling price of $18,000, a residual value of $8,000, and a lease term of 48 months. In addition, we will assume an approximate annual lease rate of 8.4% and a 5.75% sales tax. Finally, we will assume a bank loan requiring a down payment of 20%. See Table 4:2 on the following page for the comparison.

47

Table 4:2

	Lease	Loan	Cash
Security Deposit	$350	$0	$0
Down Payment (20%)	$0	$3,600	$18,000
Acquisition Fee/Origination Fee (in payment)	$200	$200	$0
5.75% Sales Tax (Included in payment)	$17/Mo.	$22/Mo.	$1,035
Total Monthly Payments*	$15,441	$18,476	$0
Net Cost of Not Investing Cash Paid Up-Front (7% interest)	$108	$468	$2,339
Total Cost of Vehicle After 48 mos. (Monthly payments + down payment + lost use of cash + disposition fee of $200)	$15,899	$22,544	$21,374
Less Market Value of Owned Vehicle or Security Deposit in year 4	<$350>	<$8,000>	<$8,000>
Total Cost of Vehicle (over 4 yrs)	**$15,549**	**$14,544**	**$13,374**

* Monthly lease payments are $321 and monthly loan payments are $385 (each including tax)

What do we learn from our example besides the fact that there are too many numbers to deal with while sitting across from an eager salesperson? Let's do the analysis and see.

48

Up Front Costs

✔Lease   Loan   Cash

Cash is nice—especially when it stays in your pocket! That is why leasing beats borrowing or paying cash as the most attractive way for people to drive a vehicle which might otherwise be beyond their immediate means. Leasing offers the opportunity to drive away without having to make a cash down payment. In our loan scenario, the total cost of making a $3,600 down payment (in terms of lost investment interest at 7%) is $467 and more than five times that amount if the customer decides to pay cash for the vehicle. Most consumers place an even higher premium on keeping their cash, and leasing frees them to spend it elsewhere. In our consumption-oriented society, being able to drive the car of your choice **and** purchase a new computer **right now** seems to be a prime motivating factor for those deciding whether to purchase or lease a vehicle.

Monthly Payments

✔Lease   Loan   Cash

No doubt, leasing gives you a better ride for your ruble. In our example, the person financing the car will pay roughly $64.00 per month more than the person leasing the vehicle, even after paying $3,600 in cash, up front, for the down payment. If the difference in monthly payment amounts does not seem all that large to you, consider that increasing the monthly lease payment from $321 to equal the $385 loan payment would permit the lessee to add nearly **$3,600** more in options and accessories. Leasing a vehicle can make the difference between driving a stripped-down version and cruising in one loaded with extras.

Taxes

✔Lease   Loan   Cash

With a lease, depending upon the state in which you live, you may not have to pay the full tax bill otherwise due in a purchase situation. In states where you pay tax only on the actual payments made during the term of your lease, you are essentially being taxed on the estimated depreciation of the vehicle and not its purchase price. This saves you money! In other states, you are taxed on the full "purchase price" equivalent, even though you may not buy it at lease end. In our example, the lessee in a tax-favorable state will pay a total of $816 in taxes while the purchaser will pay $1,046. For more information about taxes, see Chapter Ten—*Just the Tax.*

As illustrated by the three previous factors, leasing offers you the ability to leverage your vehicle acquisition in a significant way. The pronounced benefits of leasing have a powerful effect on one's decision-making process, but they are only part of the analysis. The next two factors show the advantages of purchasing.

End of the Day

Lease ✔Loan Cash

You cannot drive what you do not have. At the end of 48 months, if you leased the car, you will have nothing but canceled checks to show for your monthly payments, unless you buy the vehicle for a price far in excess of what most astute consumers would pay. On the other hand, had you financed the car in our example, you would not only own the vehicle you have been paying for, but you also would have spent roughly $1,000 less than the lessee over the same period. These facts tend to dim the luster of leasing. Moreover, while it may be convenient for a lessee to simply return the car at lease end and drive away with a brand new one, the lessee will also be driving away with a new set of car payments—something a purchaser will be free from as long as he owns the car. Generally speaking, if you get the itch for a new ride every two or three years, owning your vehicle may be a burden. On the other hand, if you are a loyal servant of your sedan and expect to own it for more than four years, buying it is probably a better option for you.

Total Cost to Drive

Lease   Loan   ✔ Cash

Provided you do not need the funds for other things, paying cash for a vehicle is usually the least expensive way to go in the long run. In our example, the total cost to drive the car paid for in cash after four years was nearly $2,200 less than the cost borne by the lessee and nearly $1200 less than that borne by the person who financed the vehicle, **even after taking into account the cash purchaser's $2,339 loss from not investing purchase dollars elsewhere.**[11] By purchasing a vehicle for cash, you can also eliminate acquisition fees, termination fees, and loan fees (the cost of pushing paper). If you do not have the free cash, or do not want to part with that much money in one shot, buying over time rather than leasing presents the second-best long term alternative.

---

[11] A precise economic analysis would take into account the present value of cash outflows under both lease and buy scenarios as well as the relatively unquantifiable value of the lessee's option to purchase. For most consumers, however, the analysis in Table 4.2 is more than adequate.

Leasing, of course, costs the most in terms of total funds spent (Paying cash might be more expensive than leasing when the value of the vehicle purchased plummets to extremely low levels after the purchase).

Other Factors

? Lease   ? Loan   ? Cash

Some other factors to consider when deciding whether to lease or buy your vehicle include,

☞   Anticipated Mileage

☞   Possibility of Terminating Early

☞   Personal or Business Use

☞   Emotional Considerations

Mileage Penalties

If you expect to drive your leased vehicle a great deal, leasing will be more costly for you than for lessees who do not. The estimated depreciation of your vehicle is based on your driving it an average of 12,000 miles per year. As a result, the more miles you expect to drive, the less your vehicle's predicted residual value will be at lease end. You will pay for this accelerated decline in value through a decrease in your residual value and corresponding increase in your monthly payment. Typical leases contain 12,000-mile annual limits. Exceeding the mileage limits on your lease can cost you between 10 and 15 cents per mile at lease end. Some independent leasing companies charge more and permit even fewer miles. Driving just 2500 miles over the limit, each year, on a four-year lease can translate into an additional $1,500. If you anticipate exceeding the given limits, it is cheaper to "buy" extra miles at the beginning of your lease when the rate works out to around $0.08 per mile. At some level (usually 90,000–100,000 for the entire lease term) the residual value becomes so difficult to predict that lessors will refuse to allow you to buy additional miles.

Early Termination

If you intend to lease a vehicle, have a long talk with yourself about whether you really want to stay in it for the entire term of the lease. If you cannot seem to tap into your feelings, get a copy of the lease you intend to sign and go to the section on early termination. After hiring a cryptographer to decipher it, you will immediately understand why leasing companies permit you to terminate early—you pay handsomely for the privilege! Keep this in mind when deciding on a suitable lease term. (See Chapter Eight— *Termination: A Clause For Concern* for a detailed discussion of the cost of early termination).

Personal or Business Use

Leasing a vehicle is often the best alternative for businesses because the Internal Revenue Service limits depreciation on owned vehicles, but liberally permits lease payments to be expensed under appropriate circumstances. The regulations governing leased vehicles are also far easier to sift through than the myriad restrictions on depreciation and deductions for owned vehicles. When deciding whether to lease or buy for your business, you should consult with your accountant for answers tailored to your business. If you are really brave, pick up a bottle of aspirin and a copy of IRS Publication 917—*Business Use of a Car.*

Emotional Considerations

Emotional considerations are obviously the most difficult factor to quantify. Yet, emotions are often the most compelling force which drives us to opt for a lease when a purchase may make more economic sense. As we have seen, leasing affords us the power to drive a nicer vehicle for less money in the short term. Consequently, when given the ability to move up to a better model or nicely appoint the model we have chosen, the temptation is great to throw rational economics out the window in favor of the desire to drive what looks and feels nicer. This is just another reason why the ultimate decision to lease or buy should be made in the calm of your family room rather than in the excitement of the showroom.

Making a
Lease Check List

5

U nless you are a walking PC, you will probably not be able to read this book, waltz into a showroom and "show the dealer a thing or two about leasing!" For most people, there are simply too many calculations to perform and variables to consider to intelligently assess a deal while sitting in the dealership. Instead of allowing the deal to close on your first visit with the dealer, you are better off taking the time to gather information for your analysis and returning on a different day. Bringing the numbers home will not only permit you to carefully analyze the deal, but it will also give you time to shop more and avoid making an ill-advised impulse purchase.

To obtain the best results at the dealership, negotiate the cap cost or purchase price first. If you know you will be leasing, I recommend getting to the cap cost immediately. Some "experts" recommend that you not disclose your intention to lease until after you have obtained what you believe is the best possible purchase price, after which you then casually mention to the dealer that you may wish to consider leasing the vehicle. In my view, this accomplishes little, unless your goal is to appear too clever—by half. In reality, there are differences in rates and promotional reductions on purchases and leases. So rather than waste both your time and the dealer's, I recommend cutting to the chase. Your candor will probably be as welcome to the dealer as his will be to you. Besides, if you have educated yourself as to the mechanics of leasing, there is no advantage in hiding the ball. In fact, by getting to the point and asking the right questions, you may actually convey to the dealer that you are an educated buyer who just needs the facts, not the pitch.

After you receive the dealer's best offer, obtain the other information described in the "List" which follows. This will give you the data necessary to crunch your quote or fully analyze it with your calculator or software such as *LeaseWizard®* in the unpressured environment of your own home.

THE LIST

1. Vehicle Information
    a. Year/Make/Model   _____
    b. Options   _____

2. Purchase Price (Capitalized Cost)
    a. MSRP (Sticker Price)   _____
    b. Dealer Discount/Rebates/
         Other Dealer Reductions   <_____>
    c. Dealer's "Best" Price   _____
    d. Your Cap Cost Reductions   _____
         i. Trade in allowance   <_____>
         ii. Down Payment   <_____>
    e. Fees "Rolled" Into Lease   _____
         i Acquisition Fee   _____
         ii Other Fees   _____
    f. Luxury Tax Amount   _____
    g. ADJ. CAP COST   _____

3. Facts Needed to Analyze Monthly Payment
    a. Quoted Monthly Payment   _____
    b. Residual Value   _____
    c. Ann. Rate or Money Factor   _____
    d. If no rate, Lease Charge   _____
    e. Sales/Use Tax Rate   _____
    f. Method of Taxation   _____

4. Other Important Information
    a. Mileage Cap   _____
    b. Excess Mileage Fee   _____
    c. Cost to "buy" extra miles   _____
    d. Disposition Fee   _____
    e. Title and Registration Fees   _____
    f. Other Fees (not in payment)   _____
    g. Security Deposit   _____

See Appendix C for additional worksheets!

Do the Work!

Verify your information. Run your calculations according to the formulae in this book or run the numbers through your leasing software. Your monthly payment should match or come very close to the number given to you by the dealer. If it does not, you may have some questions for your dealer. Check your math a few times, however, before you leap to any conclusions. Often, calculation of taxes leads to discrepancies in the numbers. If you have a large difference, have the dealer explain it thoroughly. Most dealers shoot straight, but if yours happens to deal from the bottom of the deck, your diligence will pay off.

Before You Shop

Before you begin gathering your "List" of data, consult new car guides or online pricing services so you have an idea of what to expect and what to shoot for. Check Appendix A for a list of leasing resources which provide everything from invoice pricing to residual value data. By shopping before you hit the road, your trip to the dealer will be more likely to yield positive results. If you simply detest the yin and yang negotiation, you can always try one of the finder services, like Auto-By-Tel or Car Bargains, which do the shopping for you by finding a dealer in your area offering the best deal on the vehicle you seek. (See Appendix A). Regardless of how you choose to negotiate a lower price, there really is no substitute for having the knowledge yourself. The more you know about how much you should be paying, both in a purchase and in a lease, the more likely you are to arrive at that destination.

Compare Fees

Often, the difference between two competing lease deals comes down to a few hundred dollars in up-front fees. If two dealers vying for your business have made roughly equivalent offers, don't forget to examine the small stuff like dealer prep fees, acquisition fees, destination charges and disposition fees. You may not be able to negotiate reductions in these (except for the prep fee which is usually easy pickins), but you can certainly shop for the lowest combination if two competing dealers are neck-and-neck on the major numbers. Many "experts" will advise you to negotiate the acquisition fee, for example, because they say it is "pure profit." In a sense, this is true. The acquisition fee is essentially a document preparation fee, but in virtually all cases, it is *not a fee charged by the dealer.* Rather, it is charged by the *leasing company* and either you or the dealer must pay it. Therefore, if you are skilled or tenacious enough to negotiate a reduction in the acquisition fee or eliminate it altogether, pat yourself on the back because you will have probably succeeded in getting the dealer to pick up the charge. Who knows, the dealer may be willing to take the small shave on his profit if it means putting you in one of his new vehicles instead of one of his competitors' products. After all, most dealers make their money from the sale of used vehicles and by providing service (especially warranty service). The more vehicles that dealer puts on the road, the more service he will perform and the larger his future allocations of new vehicles will be. It is also more likely that you will return to him with

65

your used car at lease end, giving him another new deal and a used car to sell. Keep this in mind when you shop the fees. It could save you a few hundred dollars.

Analyzing the Ads

_____ 6

O pen your newspaper, flip on the radio, pick up a magazine or surf through a few television stations and you are bound to be bombarded with advertisements for "super" lease deals. Invariably, these ads tout such low monthly payments and such low lease rates, that you may wonder whether the dealer will be paying you to drive the vehicle! Then, at the end of the lease advertisement, there is reality— a mind-boggling array of numbers, lease jargon, exceptions, conditions, limitations, restrictions and qualifications which, if examined closely, reveal the "less than obvious" facts about the deal advertised. Learning to spot the "bogus" deals before you travel to the dealership will save you time and disappointment. It will also sharpen your lease analysis skills for the real deal.

Here is the qualification paragraph from an advertisement appearing in a local newspaper for a 36-month lease of an Audi A6 quattro for only **$439** per month:

36-month closed-end lease offered to qualified customers by VW Credit, Inc. through participating dealers through August 31, 1995. **$2,500 down pmt., $439 1st month's pmt., $400 refundable security deposit and $450 acquisition fee due at lease inception.** Rate based on $32,435 MSRP of 1995 Audi A6 quattro Sedan inc. auto. Trans., all-weather package & destination chg., less required dealer contribution, which could affect final negotiated transaction. Other options, dealer prep., taxes, registration extra. Lessee responsible for insurance. Monthly payments total $15,804. At lease end, lessee responsible for $0.15/mile over 30,000 miles, for damage and excess wear, and for a $250 disposal fee. Option to purchase at lease end for $17,515 in example shown. See your dealer for details.

Columbus Dispatch, July 13, 1995

Unraveling the Mysteries

I have picked apart this ad in order to explain what each phrase or term means within the context of the deal. You will find similar language in other advertisements.

> *36-month closed-end lease offered to qualified customers of VW Credit, Inc. through participating dealers.*

A **closed-end lease** means that the lessor guarantees the residual value of the vehicle at the number specified in the lease. This should be contrasted with an **open-end lease** under which you would be liable for the shortfall between the agreed residual value and the actual amount received when the vehicle is sold at lease end.

VW Credit will review your credit history. If it does not meet their standards, they may refuse to give you the advertised deal. The fact that VW Credit (VW's captive finance company) is expressly mentioned suggests that the lease is subvented.

The key phrase in this sentence is "participating dealers." If your dealer is not participating in the promotion, he is not required to honor the offer.

> *$2,500 down pmt., $439 1st month pmt., $400 refundable security deposit and $450 acquisition fee due at lease inception.*

Be prepared to shell out at least $3,789 before you even touch the keys. You must make a cap cost reduction (down payment) of $2,500. This is roughly equivalent to paying an additional $70 per month, which instantly blows the advertised monthly price through the $500 ceiling. In addition, you must give the lessor a security deposit of $400, which should (but usually will not) be accruing interest for you while the lessor holds it. (At 5%, it's only $63.05, but you could probably could find some use for that money).

> *Rate based on $32,435 MSRP of Audi A6 quattro Sedan incl. auto. trans., all-weather package & destination chg., less required dealer contribution, which could affect final negotiated transaction.*

This ad is quite deceiving. It does not tell you the final adjusted capital cost of the car (the purchase price), the residual value, the lease rate or lease charges, or the required dealer contribution; so you cannot accurately determine how much you are actually paying for the car. It does tell you that in order to get the offered rate, you must take a car with the limited options specified (automatic transmission, all-weather package). In all likelihood, this will be a stripped-down "leader" model. Finally, you must pay a "destination charge." This is the cost of getting the vehicle from the manufacturer to the dealer. Find out how much this is and ask the dealer whether he must pay it if you do not. Remember, in some states, the dealer cannot legally charge you this fee if he is being reimbursed for it by the manufacturer.

Other options, dealer prep., taxes, registration extra. Lessee responsible for insurance.

The $439 monthly payment does not include additional features like leather seats, power locks, etc . . . nor does it include taxes. Even if you like the barebones model, at a 5.75% tax rate, your monthly payments will be $464, or the equivalent of $525, if you factor in the down payment. From your

71

checkbook's perspective, it doesn't much matter that the government, not the dealer, is charging you for the taxes. You will pay the tax, so you should consider it when analyzing this ad. Depending on the meaning of the phrase "Lessee responsible for insurance," you may also have to shell out extra for gap protection. Suddenly, the base model Audi is pricing out a little higher than the ad leads you to believe.

Total monthly payments of $15,804

This is simply $439 times 36 months. Your total monthly payments will be higher if you factor the taxes and extra charges into your lease, or add any options to the car.

At lease end, lessee responsible for $0.15 per mile over 30,000 miles.

This is a puny mileage allowance. Most drivers exceed 10,000 miles per year. Find out how much it will cost you up front to raise this allowance and balance that amount against the likely penalties you will incur by exceeding the allowance. At $0.08 per mile, your monthly payment just went up by at least another $13.00.

Lessee is responsible for excess wear

You tell me what this means. If the contract does not spell out what constitutes "excess wear," ask the dealer to spell it out for you.

Option to purchase at lease end for $17,515 plus a disposal fee of $250.

Boy, is this a good deal—just not for you! If you add it all up, you will have paid $2,500 down, a $450 acquisition fee, $15,804 in monthly payments, $17,515 to purchase the vehicle, and possibly a $250 disposal fee to exercise your purchase option. This totals **$34,019**. That's nearly $1,600 more than the **sticker** price! If you finance the purchase price at lease end, you wind up paying even more. Since the residual value and the lease rate are missing from the ad, you cannot tell how much profit the lessor expects to make on the sale of the vehicle to you at lease end.

Regulation M and Advertising

Recent amendments to existing federal leasing regulations, should rectify some of the problems we have witnessed with print advertisements as well as those associated with broadcast advertisements which do not give consumers the luxury of fine print to mull over.[12] In the print arena, for example, the new regulation requires that except for the monthly payment amount, no other component of the total amount due at signing may be advertised more prominently than any other component. This will prevent lessors from advertising a low or no down

---

[12] In 1994, the Riegle Community Development and Regulatory Improvement Act amended the Consumer Leasing Act to permit radio lease advertisements to contain less disclosure information. As enacted, the law permits lessors to include a toll-free number in lieu of complex disclosures, allowing consumers meaningful access to information necessary to analyze the promotion. The new Regulation M will expand that provision to include television advertisements.

payment in large print while mentioning other charges of equal or greater amounts due at lease signing in small or relatively inconspicuous print. In addition, the purchase option price must be mentioned if the consumer can purchase the vehicle at lease end. The most powerful advertising additions to Regulation M are those relating to lease rate disclosure. The Regulation now provides that if a lease rate is advertised it may not be called and annual percentage rate (or similar term) and that it must be accompanied by a warning that the rate may not be a measure of the overall cost of financing the vehicle (For a full discussion of Regulation M, see Chapter 9—*Leasing Legislation*).

NOTE: Although these amendments only apply to advertisements relating to consumer leases with cap costs of less than $25,000, it is safe to assume that most vehicle lessors will attempt to comply with the regulation in connection with higher priced vehicles.

Getting To The Pointers

_____ 7

L easing a new vehicle does not have to be an
uncomfortable experience. In fact, the more you
know about leasing, the more enjoyable shopping for
and negotiating a good deal can be. Before you accuse
me of having twisted notions of what is enjoyable,
consider that the car market is unlike any other retail
market in terms of the breadth and depth of
information and tools available to the **educated**
consumer. Mark Engram, sales manager of a
Columbus Nissan dealership from whom I recently
leased a car, put it best. He said, "you can hardly go
into a grocery store for a can of soup, find out what
the store paid for it, what its incentives were, and then
negotiate with the grocer until he sells it to you for 2
cents over invoice." And yet, with so many resources

available, that is exactly what an educated consumer can do when leasing a car. Many reputable dealers will also tell you that they welcome educated consumers who know how to negotiate intelligently and reasonably. Toward that end, the following is a recap of points to remember before embarking on your leasing adventure.

Negotiating the Best Deal

☞ Look for **subvented** lease deals! Leases that are subsidized by manufacturers are often good bargains. High residual values are usually the hallmarks of subvented deals.

☞ Don't play games if you intend to lease—tell the dealer you are interested in leasing and open the negotiations with the **cap cost.** Use pricing guides to help you in evaluating the proposed cap cost including selected options.

 ☞ Add **gap insurance** to your lease if it is not already provided. That way, if your vehicle is stolen or totaled before the end of your lease, you will not be stuck making the lease payments due through lease end (something your ordinary insurance will not cover). Typically, the cost of gap protection is no more than a few hundred dollars and it is usually included in the lease rate.

☞ Generally, avoid making a **down payment** on a lease. One of the primary benefits of a lease is that it allows you to avoid making a significant, up-front cash outlay. Do the math. The money is better off in your pocket.

☞ If you are trading in a vehicle, make sure you are getting the proper credit for your trade-in. Since leases are based on the difference between the negotiated purchase price and the residual value (a much smaller number than the purchase price), reductions in the cap cost from trade-in's (with equity) result in magnified savings on your lease payment. Review your paperwork carefully and crunch the numbers or use leasing software to make sure you are getting the credit you bargained for.

Avoid leasing a vehicle for a **term** that exceeds the manufacturer's warranty unless you are prepared to pay for repairs to a vehicle you do not own.

Know the four elements of your lease: Cap cost, lease charge (or money factor), residual value and term.

Generally, avoid enterting into an **open-end** lease. If you do sign one, it means that you, and not the lessor, will be liable for the difference between the estimated residual value and the actual value of the vehicle at lease end.

General Pointers

 Do not be pressured into signing a lease or purchase agreement on your first visit. Shop around and run the numbers. You will be amazed at the money you'll save. Use pricing guides and pricing services to help you uncover invoice prices, rebate programs and other dealer incentives which can translate into lower prices for you (See Appendix A— *Leasing Resources*).

 If you expect to pile on the miles, be sure to find out how much it costs to "buy" extra miles up front. Some companies charge as much as $.15 per mile at the back end of the lease for mileage in excess of 10,000 per year.

Leases are better on vehicles that are predicted to hold their value over the term of the lease. Remember, the higher the residual value, the lower the monthly payment. Generally, new models have higher predicted residual values at the beginning of their design cycle. Consult the ALG residual value guide to get an idea of what the baseline is for the model you are considering (See Appendix A—*Leasing Resources*).

☞ Take good care of your leased vehicle and have it cleaned thoroughly before turning it in at lease end. Your vehicle will be inspected after you return it and you will be liable for any damage to the vehicle beyond ordinary wear and tear. Inspectors are human, and a clean vehicle gives the impression that you were kind to it during the lease term, which enhances the likelihood that the inspector will "overlook" minor items that the lessor might otherwise claim as damage beyond ordinary wear and tear.

☞ Finally, do not lease a vehicle to save money. If you do, you should be beaten soundly with

"The Club." Leasing almost always costs more in the long run, even if the monthly payments are less than those on a purchase.

Early Termination:
A Clause For Concern

8
_____

If you are leaning toward leasing your next vehicle, ask yourself whether you intend to drive it for the full term of the lease. If you suspect that you may terminate the lease early, think twice about even leasing at all. Terminating a vehicle lease early is a costly proposition—if you can do it. Most leases have a termination clause, but some only permit you to exercise your right after a certain number of months have elapsed. If you terminate early, at the very least you should expect to pay:

$ an early termination fee (usually between $250 and $400),

$ any past-due payments,

$ the present value of all future payments due under the lease (discounted at the lease rate) and

$ a early termination penalty.

Against these charges, the lessee typically receives credit for the difference between the present value of the residual value and the current value of the vehicle. Here is a simplified example.

Assume that the lessee of a 15,000 car (with a $7,000 residual value), terminates a 48-month lease after making 12 monthly payments of $250. Assume, further, that the leasing company auctions the vehicle for $10,000. Under a typical default provision, the lessee would be responsible for future lease payments of $9,000 (36 more payments times $250), a $350 disposition fee plus an early termination penalty of $300. From this initial liability of $9,650, the lessee is given credit for the $3,000 in sale proceeds received by the lessor over and above the vehicle's residual value ($10,000 less $7,000). This leaves the lessee with a liability of **$6,650** and **no car!** It is hard to think of a more effective deterrent to early termination. If you think you've seen enough, look at what the lessor receives:

- $3,000 in payments for the first year,

- $6,650 in termination costs from the lessee,

  and

- $10,000 from the sale of the vehicle

for a total of **$19,350** after only one year under the lease. Even though this figure is essentially what the lessor bargained to receive over the life of the lease, the point is that the lessor received that money all in one year instead of over four years. Moreover, if the lessee is not given credit for the difference between the current value and the residual value, the lessor will have received a windfall of $3,000 plus whatever the lessor can make by investing that money for three years. In addition to these pleasant consequences, some leases charge the lessee for all taxes due under the remainder of the lease.

One of the reasons why early termination is such an ugly alternative relates to the credit you receive on the lessor's sale of your vehicle. Since the vehicle will be sold in the **wholesale** market, you will not receive as much credit against your termination liability as you would have had your vehicle been sold for its retail value. To add to your losses, the residual value (which is subtracted from the low sale price to figure your credit) is probably an inflated estimate designed to keep your monthly payments down, so you lose on both ends of the equation.

Perhaps the most insidious problem with early termination clauses is their outright complexity. Termination clauses are notoriously confusing. But don't take my word for it. The following is an excerpt from an early termination clause found in a lease form used by a captive finance company (I will call them AMAC) in 1993:

This Lease may be terminated by the Lessee before the end of the term if the Lessee is not in default under this Lease, gives AMAC and the Lessor **10** days written notice, delivers the Vehicle to the Lessor and pays to Lessor at once the following: (a) an early termination fee of **$350**, (b) the difference, if any between the Adjusted Balance Subject to Lease Charges and the Realized Value of the Vehicle, and (c) all other amounts then due under this Lease. The Adjusted Balance Subject to Lease Charges will be figured by reducing the Balance Subject to Lease Charges each month by the difference between the Monthly Payment (Item 2(a) on reverse side) and the part of the Lease Charges (Item 15 on reverse side) earned in that month on an actuarial basis. The Balance Subject to Lease Charges shall be calculated by adding the Lease Residual Value (Item 16 on reverse side) to the Lease Depreciation. The Lease Depreciation shall be calculated by subtracting (y) the Lease Charges (Item 15 on reverse side) from (z) the amount of the Monthly Payments (Item 2(a) on reverse side) multiplied by the Lease term in months (Item 5 on the reverse side).

Now take a breath. Not surprisingly, there is little room for confusion about sub-part (a) which boldly proclaims the early termination fee of $350. Likewise, sub-part (c) makes it clear that the lessee will owe all amounts then due at termination. After that, the road becomes treacherous. As a lawyer, I found the rest of this provision extremely perplexing (perhaps because it was written by one of my collegues!). So imagine the difficulty that most consumers will have while trying to assess the cost of terminating early if they have a lease with this or a similar clause.

Under the Federal Consumer Leasing Act in force at the time, leases of vehicles costing less than $25,000 were required to contain termination clauses in "a reasonably understandable form." Do you think AMAC's clause made the grade? I did not and I challenged the company on their language because I was looking to terminate my leases on two vehicles they were leasing me at the time. After a pointed letter and a few phone calls, I was able to negotiate a waiver of the disposition fee, waiver of the purchase option fee and a cash reduction in the termination liability. In all, I saved about $3,000 on both leases. Of course, AMAC never admitted that there was anything wrong with its termination clause. Fortunately, AMAC has since changed its lease form and clarified its termination language.

Interestingly, the new Regulation M does little to dictate to how understandable termination language must be. That means the courts will be called upon to determine, on a case-by-case basis, whether or not a particular termination clause is so unintelligible that a violation of the Consumer Leasing Act has occurred. For the average consumer, the best bet is to read the contract and ask questions **before** you sign the lease because most lessors will stand by the existing language of their contracts and it is unlikely that you will be able to negotiate a reduction in your termination liability based on a challenge of the lease language.

The bottom line: Prepare to stay in your lease or pay for exiting early. The first option is easier and usually much cheaper!

Leasing Legislation

9

As the popularity of leasing grew throughout the 90's, so did the incidence of fraud and abuse in the industry. The Florida Attorney General documented fraud and overcharging in nearly 10% of all new vehicle leases over a 24-month study. Other states documented similar rates of abuse. The abuse was due, in large part, to consumers' ignorance of the leasing process. By knowing only how much they were paying per month, unwary consumers had no idea if they were grossly overpaying for their vehicles or whether they were paying too much in lease charges. This left the door wide open for unscrupulous dealers to take unfair advantage of consumers.

In response to the growing epidemic of abuse, attorneys general and consumer advocate groups across the country mounted a campaign for full and fair disclosure of all essential elements of a lease. In late 1993, the Federal Reserve Board focused on the problem and began to craft changes to Regulation M (regulations to the Consumer Leasing Act, a law originally enacted in 1976 as an amendment to the Truth in Lending Act - 15 U.S.C. §1601 for you law junkies). Although the Consumer Leasing Act and its accompanying regulations provided some disclosures to make leasing a clearer process for consumers, the Federal Reserve Board recognized that changes and supplementation were necessary in order to fulfill the purpose behind the law—full and uniform disclosure.

The Federal Reserve slogged along for two years before members of the Association of Consumer Vehicle Lessors took steps of their own in the summer of 1995 by agreeing to begin disclosing the capitalized cost of leased vehicles in their form lease agreements. Their action was a voluntary and perhaps preemptive response to growing pressure from consumer and governmental inquiry. Since most of the nation's large captive finance companies are members of the ACVL, the benefits of their voluntary action were expected to become widespread once their program was fully implemented by each member. Before this voluntary reform would sweep the industry, however, the Federal Reserve Board finally acted on September 27, 1996 when it approved final amendments to Regulation M.[13] Having the benefit of extensive comments from the public, the leasing industry and consumer groups, the final regulations incorporate the essence of the ACVL voluntary changes and more.

---

[13] Commentary to Regulation M will be finalized on April 1, 1997. Commentary to the Regulation is important because the Federal Reserve Board's clarifying explanations will give consumers and lessors alike an even better understanding of how the Regulation will be interpreted and enforced.

Regulation M—How Does it Work?

To break it down into its simplest and most important components, we offer the following bullet-point list of its features. This summary includes both new and existing elements of Regulation M to give you a complete picture of what protections will be available as of October 1997 when the regulation goes into effect (for those who cannot seem to get enough law, the full text, including selected forms, is reprinted in Appendix B).

Leases Covered

- Only applies to "consumer leases." This means leases by *individuals* for personal, family or household purposes which exceed 4 months in length. Regulation M does **not** apply to leases for agricultural, business or commercial purposes **or** leases made to an organization.

- Only applies to leases with a total contractual obligation equal to or less than **$25,000**. That's right, if you leased a luxury car, almost any sport utility vehicle, or even a mid-priced touring sedan, you are technically out of luck under Regulation M. Nonetheless, it is unlikely that leasing companies will develop two sets of lease forms—one that complies with Regulation M for vehicles less than $25,000 and one that does not for more expensive vehicles. In that sense, most, if not all, consumers should benefit by the new rules. You also may be protected if your state has its own legislation.[14]

How Disclosures Must be Made

● Most of the required disclosures must be segregated from the rest of the lease. Interestingly, the new regulation eliminated a previous requirement that they also be printed

---

[14]Given the rising cost of automobiles, this author would not be surprised to see a legislative amendment to the Consumer Leasing Act making it applicable to vehicles with an adjusted capitalized cost in excess of $25,000 (The Federal Reserve Board is legally prohibited from making a change of that type).

in the equivalent of 10-point or larger type or legibly handwritten.

• Disclosures must be given to consumers all at the same time and before the lease is executed.

What Must be Disclosed

✔ A **description** of the leased property

✔ **The total amount of money due at lease signing, itemized by the type of charge.** This requirement forces the lessor to list exactly how much you are being asked to pay for each item, such as security deposit, first monthly payment and down payment. It also requires the lessor to reflect credit for trade-in allowances, rebates or other discounts.

✔ **Other Charges** This new addition requires disclosure of any additional charges such as a disposition fee or other lease-end liabilities.

✔ **Total of Payments** Although the heading suggests only a disclosure of the total of all monthly payments, this provision actually requires the lessor to give the total of **all amounts spent** by the lessee, including, amounts due at lease signing, and other charges (in open-end leases, an additional disclosure regarding lease-end liability is required).

✔ **Monthly payment information.** This includes the number, amount and due dates for payments under the lease as well as the total of all monthly payments.

✔ **Payment Calculation** This is a useful one! The lease must give a step-by-step mathematical explanation of how the monthly payment was derived. (See Appendix B for the Federal Reserve Board's Model Closed-End Lease

Disclosure form). The calculation must include the following items:

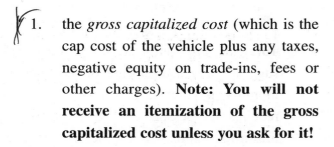

1. the *gross capitalized cost* (which is the cap cost of the vehicle plus any taxes, negative equity on trade-ins, fees or other charges). **Note: You will not receive an itemization of the gross capitalized cost unless you ask for it!**

2. any *capitalized cost reductions,*

3. the resulting *adjusted capitalized cost,*

4. the *residual value*

5. the *depreciation* plus any amounts to be "financed" or "rolled" into the lease.

6. the total *lease charge*

7. total of monthly payments

8. lease *term*

9. the monthly sales tax

10.   the monthly payment

11.   other charges included in payment

✔   **Early termination** Regulation M will require a statement of the conditions under which the lessee may terminate early, the cost or method of determining the cost of early termination and the penalty or other charge imposed for early termination. The new regulation also requires the lessor to give a warning to the effect that charges for early termination may be substantial and that the charges will be higher the earlier one elects to terminate. **The problem with this amendment is that it does not address the problem of complex and incoherent termination clauses.**

✔   **Maintenance responsibilities** The lessor must indicate who is responsible for maintaining or servicing your vehicle (usually you!).

Wear and tear If the manufacturer has a standard for wear and tear, it must be disclosed. Otherwise, you will receive a simple warning that you will be charged for wear in excess of what the company considers "normal." This one is puzzling because it allows the lessor to set no standard and disclose nothing, leaving the lessee to guess what will constitute excessive wear and tear. (The best advice is to take good care of your leased vehicle!). Included in the wear and tear provision is a requirement that the lessor disclose the cost of exceeding your mileage limits under the lease.

✔ **Purchase Option** The lease must indicate whether you have the option to purchase and if so at what price.

✔ **Fees payable** This includes the total amount payable for official fees, registration, certificate of title, license fees or taxes.

✔ **All other charges not included in the monthly payment.** This includes fees payable at lease end (i.e. disposition fee, purchase option fee). It does not include the difference between the estimated and actual realized value at the end of an open end lease.

 Insurance information. The lease form should indicate the types of insurance and coverage amounts provided by the lessor as well as those not provided by the lessor but required by the lessee.

✔ **Warranties.** The lease must disclose what warranties are available to the lessee under the lease.

✔ **Liens, if any.** The lease must disclose any assets (including the vehicle) against which the lessor is taking a lien.

✔ **Penalty Information.** The lease should disclose the amount or the formula for calculating the amount of any penalties for late payments or other defaults.

✔ **Open-End Liability.** If the lease is an open-ended lease, there is a host of disclosures regarding the right of appraisal and the calculation of lease end liability.

Where is the Lease Rate Disclosure?

Noticeably absent from Regulation M is a mandatory lease rate disclosure provision requiring the lessor to indicate the lease rate or money factor. The regulation only states that **if** the lessor chooses to provide a percentage rate in an advertisement or in the lease documents, he must also provide a warning stating: *"this percentage may not measure the overall cost of financing this lease."* At first blush, this might seem like a gaping oversight by the Federal Reserve Board or the result of political football playing among the more

104

powerful members of the leasing industry. You may be surprised to know that exclusion of lease rate information from the list of required disclosures actually has merit.

The Legal Hurdle ("Separation of Powers 101")

Since Regulation M was crafted by a non-legislative body (the Federal Reserve Board) as a tool to enforce an existing statute (Truth and Lending Act), that body cannot legally create obligations and restrictions which were not originally intended by the underlying statute. That is a job left to the legislative body that crafted the law. As a result, the Federal Reserve Board lacks the authority to require lease finance companies to disclose lease rates, which arguably do not fall within the types of disclosures originally contemplated by the Truth and Lending Act. Accordingly, short of an amendment or new law enacted by Congress, the Federal Reserve Board cannot legally require rate disclosures as part of Regulation M. Rather than risk having its entire regulation tied up in the court system, the Federal Reserve Board wisely chose not to tread beyond the bounds of its authority by mandating lease rate disclosure. But this was not their only rationale for excluding lease rates from the list of disclosures. There are substantive reasons for not requiring lease rate disclosure which figured in the Federal Reserve Board's decision.

The Unnatural Nature of Lease Rates

In simplest terms, a lease rate is the rate of return realized by the lessor on its investment in the lease. In its purest form, the lease rate is simply a reflection of the return on the lessors' money. In the real world, however, there are often other charges mixed into the lease rate, such as disposition fees, purchase option fees, gap insurance premiums and purchase option mark-ups. If you include these charges in your calculations, the effective lease rate is actually higher than the return on capital the lessor is receiving. The problem is that each lessor may choose what to include in the rate and what to exclude. The result is a lack of uniformity among dealers and the resulting inability of consumers to make accurate comparisons. The difficulty in disclosing a uniform rate also stems from the fact that different residual values on the same vehicle with the same advertised monthly payment will result in different effective lease rates.

To illustrate the problem, consider a closed-end 36-month lease of an $18,000 car with an $8,000 residual value and total lease charges of $5,000. Your monthly payments (excluding taxes and fees) would be $416.66.

Example 9:1

a. $10,000   + $5,000   = $15,000
   Depreciation   Lease Charges   Total Payments

b. $15,000   ÷   36   = $416.66
   Total Payments   Term   Monthly Payment

If the dealer reduced the residual value by $3,000 from $8000 to $5,000 (increasing your payment) but simultaneously reduced the lease charges by an equal amount (decreasing your payment), your payment would not change.

Example 9:2

a. $13,000   + $2,000   = $15,000
   Depreciation   Lease Charges   Total Payments

b. $15,000   ÷   36   = $416.66
   Total Payments   Term   Monthly Payment

Even though your monthly payment has not changed, what has changed is the dealer's ability to advertise an extremely low lease rate. You may go to that dealer and cut your deal based upon the low apparent rate, never knowing that a competing dealer was offering a true lease rate lower than the one offered by your dealer before the manipulation of numbers took place. Worse, the dealer with the low lease rate may goose up the capitalized cost, even if only by a small amount, and still leave a relatively uneducated consumer with the perception that his deal is the best based on a very low lease rate.

Could you figure out whether or not you were getting the best deal from your dealer if you carefully shopped the other dealers? Sure. But, you would have to be very facile with the numbers involved and the concepts of leasing. The bottom line is that for every educated, capable leasing consumer there are thousands who would not even know to investigate these arcane aspects of the lease. From the perspective of the Federal Reserve Board, requiring dealers to disclose the lease rate would simply invite this type of numerical manipulation and undermine the purpose of the disclosure.

As a practical matter, until some uniform method of calculating lease rates is agreed upon in the industry, it is unlikely that any federal laws will be implemented to require lease rate disclosure. The same is true on the state level. In Minnesota, for example, the Attorney General recently investigated a newspaper advertisement which boasted a 4.9% lease rate in large print and in the small disclaimer said that the lease had a "4.9% APR." On its face, the rate appeared in the ad to be comparable to rates offered on vehicle loans or other vehicle leases. After investigating the dealer who ran the ad, as well as other dealers and leasing companies, the attorney general found that advertised lease rates were, across the board, about two percentage points lower than the effective annual rates actually being charged. The result: Minnesota now prohibits the advertisement or promotion of any expression of the cost of money under a lease until a generally accepted standard is adopted.

The States May Still Go Marching On

Even amid the activity by the Federal Reserve Board, the ACVL and Rep. John LaFalce, who introduced leasing reform legislation in the United States House of Representatives in May 1996, individual states have taken matters into their own hands. To the extent that laws passed by individual states do not conflict with existing federal law, they are just as enforceable as federal statutes and regulations. In many cases, laws passed by individual states have a sharper bite than the existing requirements of Regulation M.

In view of certain limitations in the scope of Regulation M, it will not be surprising to see even more states passing their own leasing legislation within the next few years. As of our publication date, several states, including, Florida, New York, New Jersey, Maine, Maryland, Washington and Wisconsin had enacted mandatory lease disclosure laws of varying scope.

New York—A Tough Apple

For lessors, New York presents the greatest challenges in crafting appropriate lease forms, making required disclosures and formulating non-misleading advertisements. The New York Motor Vehicle Leasing Act provides a comprehensive consumer

111

protection law which, among other things, requires lessors to make a blank sample copy of their lease forms available to consumers and disclose to lessees on a separate sheet of paper the fact that gap insurance is not provided under the contract (if that is the case). The statute has enforcement provisions which should provide ample incentive for leasing companies in New York to comply with the rigors of the law.

The Law Helps Those . . .

Although disclosure laws and regulations will improve the consumer's lot in leasing, without a solid nuts and bolts understanding of the concepts, disclosures will be of little or no value. Getting the information is only part of the battle. Knowing what it means and what to do with it is far more important. In other words, don't rely on the government to see you through your transaction. Be diligent and rely on nobody but yourself. Learn the ropes and you won't be left hanging!

Just the Tax

10

A s taxing as it may be to your psyche, a discussion of taxes within the context of this book is just as important as other aspects of leasing, unless you happen to be fortunate enough to hail from a state like Oregon, which has seen the wisdom in assessing NO sales tax on vehicle sales or leases. For the rest of us unfortunate souls, this chapter will explore the two prevailing methods of state lease taxation, as well as federal luxury taxes and a neat federal tax break for lessees of certain vehicles.

The Methods

There are essentially two methods of assessing sales tax in a lease transaction. The most popular method is to tax the lessee on the actual payments made under the lease. The second method imposes a tax on the entire capitalized cost of the vehicle, even though the lessee does not own the vehicle. In theory, calculating your tax under either of these methods should not be difficult. Of course, in reality, this proves less than true. Each state has not only its own general method of calculating sales tax, but also a list of taxable and nontaxable components of a lease. For now, we will explore the fundamental methods of taxation.

Stream of Payments Method

Most states use the "stream of payments" method to calculate sales tax under a lease. To figure out your tax liability under this method, just multiply your monthly payment by the tax rate plus one.

Example 10:1

Assuming your sales tax rate is .0575 (or 5.75%), and your monthly payment excluding sales tax is $339.16, your monthly payment with tax would be:

Monthly Payment	x	(1 + Tax)	=	Total Payment
$339.16	**x**	**1.0575**	**=**	**$358.66**

In addition to tax on the monthly payment, you must also pay tax on any cash down payment made because this is effectively a "purchase down" of the price of the vehicle and would not be captured in the monthly payment calculation. Just in case you were wondering, under this method you **do** pay tax on the "interest" portion of your monthly payment. Think about that one for a while.

With the stream of payments method, you do end up paying less tax than someone who leases the same vehicle in a state which taxes the full capitalized cost of the vehicle (assuming you do not purchase the vehicle at lease end). Essentially, you are paying tax only on what you are using.

Capitalized Cost Method

The capitalized cost method of taxation taxes the lessee on the capitalized cost of the vehicle and the total tax is usually payable at the commencement of the lease. This method of taxation is required in a handful of states including, Arkansas, Illinois, Iowa, Maryland, Montana, North Dakota, Oklahoma, South Dakota, and Texas. Each state has its own variations on what is included in the purchase price, and at least one state (Kentucky) defines gross purchase price as 90% of the sticker price. The lesson here is to know the precise method of taxation used by your states.

Hybrid States (if it's not one thing—it's another!)

There are certain states whose taxation scheme has characteristics of both the stream-of-payments and capitalized cost methods of taxation. In Maine, for example, lessees must pay their tax all at once at the time of acquisition. The amount, however, is calculated principally on the sum of all monthly payments, making it similar to a stream of payments state.[15] In Vermont, a tax is imposed up front on the difference between the capitalized cost and the residual value, giving the tax characteristics of both methods.

Lessor's Choice

In some states, the lessor (not the dealer) may choose the method of taxation which it will utilize with all vehicles leased in that state. It may collect and remit to the state all of the tax up front or collect and remit tax as paid monthly by the lessee.

What Exactly is Subject to the Tax?

In addition to your total purchase price or cash down payment and monthly lease payment, there are other taxable elements of your vehicle transaction. In some states, such as Maine, Michigan, Maryland and Massachusetts (no kidding!) you will be taxed on the equity in your trade-in vehicle. On the other hand,

---

[15] Unlike most stream states Maine also requires the lessee to pay tax on any equity in a trade-in.

there are many states which will not tax trade-ins provided the parties agree to the value of the vehicle being traded. Other typical lease items subject to taxation include:

- ✎ Acquisition Fees
- ✎ License Fees
- ✎ Excess Mileage
- ✎ Excess Wear and Tear
- ✎ Termination Fees
- ✎ Disposition Fees
- ✎ Collection and Repossession Fees
- ✎ Federal Luxury Tax

Noticed that Federal Luxury Tax was listed as an item on which you may be required to pay sales tax. Indeed, many states apply sales tax to the Federal Luxury Tax because the tax is as much a cost of driving the vehicle as any other component in the list.

Federal Luxury Tax

The federal government charges a luxury tax of on every dollar of a vehicle purchase price or lease capital cost (excluding fees) that exceeds $36,000. The rate, which dropped from 10% to 9% in August of 1996 and another point to 8% beginning in 1997, is scheduled to fade out in 2002. Until then, you should be aware of it if you intend to purchase a vehicle with a price in excess of $36,000. Here's how it works:

Assume you are going to lease a $44,000 vehicle, including prep and delivery fees. Since Uncle Sam gets 8% of every dollar over $36,000, your luxury tax bill will be $640 (8% of $8,000) in this case. The $640 will be tacked right onto the capital cost of the vehicle, making it $42,640. Fortunately for luxury car buyers, the threshold for luxury tax increases along with the consumer price index and the tax rate decreases one percentage point each year until 2002 when it disappears completely.

Take a Break!

Believe it or not, the Internal Revenue Code also provides a tax break for business purchasers and lessees of vehicles which exceed 6,000 lbs. empty. Since some utility vehicles exceed this weight, those of us who are not in the trucking business may find ourselves on the favorable side of this tax law. Before you get too excited, however, check with your accountant. The exception applies to the method of depreciation normally applicable to cars and works to your benefit by treating the utility vehicle as a truck, provide you meet the other requirements.

Used Car Leasing

11

As the popularity of new vehicle leasing has increased, so has the number of used, late-model cars and trucks returning to lessors and dealer lots everywhere. In response, the leasing industry has opened the door to broad-based used car leasing. What began as a handful of manufacturer-driven used car lease programs with luxury cars and sport utility vehicles, has grown into a substantial business, attracting most of the major auto manufacturers and a sizable cadre of independent leasing companies. As leasing continues to grow, experts expect used car leasing to gain in popularity not only in the luxury and sport utility markets, but among customers of mid-priced vehicles as well. According to CNW Marketing Research, nearly 500,000 used vehicles will be leased in 1996. That's more than 8% of all leases and nearly 3% of all vehicle acquisitions! The number is expected to grow to more than one million by 1999. The primary growth impetus will be consumer awareness. According to a recent CNW survey, nearly 72% of those surveyed knew that leases were available on new vehicles. Amazingly, only 14% were aware that they could lease a used vehicle.[16] As that figure increases, so will the popularity of used vehicle leases.

---

[16] You may find it disturbing (as I did) to know that among those surveyed by CNW, there were more people who knew about new vehicle leasing than those who could name the President! Go figure.

What's the Difference Between a New and Used Car Lease?

The two main differences between new and used car leases are the money factor and the rate of depreciation the vehicle will experience over the course of the lease. On one hand, a gently used vehicle (2 years) depreciates less during the next two or three years than it did during its initial two years. That saves you money. On the other hand, the money factor or lease rate in a used lease transaction is almost uniformly higher than that used on the same vehicle when it was new. Let's take a closer look at both factors.

The Depreciation Factor

In the first two years of an average car lease, the vehicle will usually depreciate by more than 40%! Over the next two years, the vehicle may decline by less than 20%. If the car is leased new for only two years, the next driver has the opportunity to lease it used and experience 50% less depreciation than his predecessor. If the car is in good condition and the body design has not changed radically, this has the makings of a good deal! Remember, the less depreciation, the smaller the difference will be between the capitalized cost and the residual value. That translates into lower payments! Be careful though, after the vehicle is four to five years old, the depreciation begins to accelerate again for most makes and models. You can track anticipated depreciation in used cars by consulting the Automotive Lease Guide's Used Car Residual Value data (See Appendix A—*Leasing Resources*).

The Residual Value Factor

What drives the value of a used vehicle lease down the most is the vehicle's residual value. Remember the high residual value you saw on the new model you considered? Forget about it in the land of pre-owned vehicles. Betting on their ability to move previously leased vehicles in the used car market, new car lessors can often afford the luxury of offering artificially high residual values to drive down monthly payments and move inventory. The same game cannot be played once a vehicle enters the used vehicle market, where artificially inflating its residual value just to lease it again, only delays the inevitable hit that the lessor will absorb when the chicken comes home to roost. **The bottom line:** Without the ability to really pump used car residual values, lessors have a difficult time offering used car leases with payments significantly more appealing than those on new vehicles.

The Money Factor—Factor

What you may save in less severe depreciation on a used vehicle lease is, in many cases, swallowed up by a higher money factor. The higher money factor is typical of used vehicles and indicates a higher level of risk for the lessor in the transaction. The higher rate gives the lessor both a return on his money and compensation for the risk of loss on resale in the event of default or at lease end. Since the salability of a used car coming off of a two-year lease is more difficult to predict than that of a new car leased for an equal term, lessors must hedge by increasing the money factor. Predictability is the key. Based upon model history and the estimated price of new models several years hence, a lessor can get a pretty good idea of what a new vehicle will be worth at any point during the term of the transaction.[17] The used car lessor does not have that luxury.

Is Used Car Leasing a Good Deal?

The answer is, "it depends!" During the relatively brief history of used vehicle leasing, there have been many instances in which the monthly cost of leasing a used vehicle is only a few bucks less than the cost of leasing the same vehicle new! That happens when a captive finance company promotes an extremely high residual value accompanied by a

---

[17] According to CNW, the value of a used vehicle increases 75¢ for every $1.00 increase in the price of the new model. Therefore, automobile companies, who know in advance the suggested price of their new models, have a very good idea of what the residual value of their current models will be when the newer models come out.

low lease rate. In those cases, the answer is obvious—go with a new lease. For most people, saving $10–$30 per month on a used vehicle is not enough to turn their attention away from a brand new version of the same make and model. In many cases, however, used vehicle leases can give consumers the same leverage a new lease has over a purchase. In other words, when you cannot afford to buy or lease that shiny new Infiniti, you may be able to lease a used one with virtually the same styling and warranties as you would have received with the new model. Unfortunately, there is no across-the-board answer. The best advice is to shop your lease and follow the hints given below.

Shopping the Used Vehicle Lease

When shopping a used vehicle lease you should do the following:

☞ Find out the cost of leasing the same model new! Use it for comparison purposes. You may be pleasantly surprised.

☞ Find a vehicle that has been owned or leased for no more than 36 months. Remember, you are not buying the car, and the length of prior ownership is important in determining how fast the value of the vehicle will decline while you are leasing it (in other words—the residual value). A vehicle previously used for 24 months is usually the best bet.

☞ Check the mileage already on the car. If the mileage exceeds 15,000 per year, the predicted residual value at the end of your term may be lower than the norm, yielding you a higher monthly payment.

☞ Make sure the vehicle has a **manufacturer's certification.** This is different from a dealer's certification, which is usually only good for getting warranty work performed at that dealership. A manufacturer's certification will usually permit you to get service work performed at any dealer who sells that vehicle make. If you have decided on a particular vehicle make, your manufacturer warranty options will not vary from dealer to dealer. However, if you are considering vehicles of different makes, be sure to compare warranties. Most of the major auto makers now have certification programs.

☞ Shop the residual values. To get a good idea of residual values, you can consult the Automotive Lease Guide, NADA guides or the Kelley Blue Book Residual Value Guide. Just look up your vehicle using its model year and see where it will be at the end of your lease term. Subtract that value from the capitalized cost being charged by the lessor and that will give you some idea of the depreciation you'll be financing under your lease.

☞ Shop the lease rates. You can shop lease rates simply by comparing the rates of one leasing company to those of another on the same vehicle. As used car leasing increases in popularity, so will the number of independent lessors, manufacturers and lending institutions competing for your dollar. This will help you.

☞ Run the calculations just as you would on a new lease and make sure your lease agreement has the same protections.

☞ **Keep your term less than 36 months!** Make the term shorter if the car is more than two years old when you lease it. Because the value of the car will decline at an increasing rate beginning around the fifth year, the benefits of the used car lease will begin to erode if your term takes you beyond that benchmark. Obviously, you should keep the length of your lease equal to or shorter than the duration of your warranties.

The Language of Leasing

12

I f you think lawyers have cornered the market on a language of their own, go lease a car. Terms used in the leasing industry can be confusing enough to make you want to hire a lawyer. Yet, without an adequate understanding of the language of leasing, it can be difficult, if not impossible, to shop for and negotiate a favorable deal for yourself. This chapter should serve as a handy reference to the terms used in the world of vehicle leasing

TERM	TRANSLATION
Acquisition Fee	Similar to a *loan fee* used to cover administrative costs of the lessor.

Adjusted Capitalized Cost	The final capital cost, including fees. See the definition of Capitalized Cost.
APR	*Annual Percentage Rate.* A term codified by federal consumer protection legislation. In simplest terms, it means the interest rate for one year charged on the unpaid balance of a loan. APR is not applicable to leases. Sometimes APR is used interchangeably with the concept of lease charges. There is a distinction between the two and APR should only be used in connection with vehicle loans.
Capitalized Cost	The purchase price of the vehicle and the amount from which the residual value will be subtracted to determine the vehicle's expected depreciation

over the term of the lease. This is not necessarily the suggested retail price of the vehicle, but rather, the negotiated price. The final capital cost, including fees, is usually referred to as the Adjusted Capitalized Cost.

Cap Cost Reduction

A reduction in the capitalized cost in the form of a cash down payment, a trade-in allowance, rebate or dealer discount.

Captive Finance Company

A leasing or finance company which is affiliated with an automobile manufacturer.

Closed-End Lease

A lease which allows the lessee to return the vehicle at the end of the lease term with no additional liability for the shortfall between the actual value of the vehicle at lease end and the projected residual value stated in the lease. In a closed-end lease, the lessor essentially guarantees the future value of the vehicle.

Dealer Discount Any amount which the dealer contributes to reduce the manufacturer's suggested retail price (sticker price or MSRP).

Depreciation A vehicle's decline in value over the term of the lease.

Disposition Fee A fee charged by most lessors to cover the expense of preparing and reselling (or auctioning) a leased vehicle at the end of the lease.

Gap Protection Insurance which is purchased to supplement conventional vehicle insurance. Gap protection (or gap insurance) covers the money you owe under the lease (future payments, fees) if the vehicle is totaled or stolen before the end of the lease.

Initiation Fee   Same as an acquisition fee.

Lease Rate   An expression of the cost of money and perhaps other charges in the lease agreement. Often stated in terms of total lease charges or monthly lease charges rather than as a rate (as the name implies).

Lessee   The individual or company that uses the vehicle.

Lessor   The individual or company that purchases the vehicle and leases it to the lessee.

Money Factor A small fraction which is used to calculate the lease charges. When multiplied by 2400, the money factor very closely approximates the equivalent annual percentage rate of interest being charged on a lease.

MSRP *Manufacturer's Suggested Retail Price.* Also known as the "sticker price."

Open-End Lease A lease which requires the lessee to make up any shortfall between the actual value of the vehicle at lease end and the projected residual value stated in the lease. In an open-end lease, the lessee essentially guarantees the future value of the vehicle at lease end. **Note:** Regulation M creates a rebuttable presumption that the consumer's liability under an open-end lease as unreasonable if it is more than three times the amount of the monthly payment.

Residual Value   The estimated value of a leased vehicle at the end of the lease term.

Subvented Lease   A lease which is subsidized, usually by the manufacturer's captive finance company.

Trade-In Allowance   The credit given to a buyer or lessee for a vehicle traded in.

Leasing Resources

Appendix A

The following is a handy list of resources, both written and electronic, that you can access in your hunt for a good lease deal. The first part of this resource list is made up of books, faxback lines, software and telephone services and is broken down by information type. The second part is a listing of Internet sites which offer various types of information.

Conventional Sources

- **Pricing Guides**

  Buy-Rite Pricing Guides
  Gives invoice prices on all makes and models including options. Buy-Rite's format is easy to

follow and includes insightful articles from nationally recognized automotive expert, John R. White. Available at a local library or bookstore. **Price: $7.95**

Pace New Car Buyer's Guide
Gives invoice prices on all makes and models including options. Available at a local library or bookstore. **Price: around $8.95.**

• **Rebate and Incentives**

Car Deals Rebate and Incentive Report
Gives consumer and dealer incentives, holdbacks and rebates for all makes and models. Available by credit card at 1-202-347-7283. **Price: $4.50.**

Fighting Chance
This company will fax you rebate and incentive information in addition to pricing information

about the vehicles you are interested in. You can also get pricing information from them. Available by credit card at 1-800-288-1134. **Price: $12.00 and up depending on the number of vehicles examined.**

• **Residual Values**

Automotive Lease Guide
Published six times annually, this is **the** guide to residual values in the industry. You may purchase the guide in written or electronic form (Windows or DOS). **Price: $120.00 for a one-year subscription (ask for their distribution agent if you are interested only in a single issue). Phone: 805.563.0777 New values are also available free over the Internet at www.residualvalue.com.**

Kelley Blue Book Residual Value Guide
Published six times annually, this guide gives you residual values in the industry for all makes

and models. Available at your local library or
by credit card at 1-800-BLUEBOOK. **Price:
$52.95 for a one-year subscription.**

- **Shopping/Locator Services**

  These services should be distinguished from
  auto brokers, who actually purchase vehicles
  and then resell or release them to you. An auto
  locator or shopping service will find you the
  best deal for a fee or for free and you must then
  purchase or lease the vehicle from the dealer or
  lessor.

  Auto-By-Tel
  Auto-By-Tel is a relatively new company in the
  shopping business, but because of its Internet
  exposure is rapidly growing and should be
  servicing all 50 states by the time this book
  reaches bookstores. Auto-By-Tel claims to be
  able to find the lowest price dealer in your area.
  You do not have to pay them for their service.
  They get paid by subscribing dealer members

who, according to Auto-By-Tel, must meet certain standards in order to remain at the "top" of the list of dealers they recommend in your area. Although my personal experience with Auto-By-Tel was less than satisfying, there are many satisfied customers who would highly recommend their service. In the end, there is no risk in contacting them over the Internet. After a few days, you will get a call from the dealer in your area who Auto-By-Tel claims is the lowest price dealer. If the dealer is the best, you've done well. If not, no harm and nothing lost but a few days. **Web: www.autobytel.com**

Car Bargains
Car Bargains is a car shopping service sponsored by the Center for the Study of Services, a purportedly non-profit organization based in Washington, D.C. But, don't let the "non-profit" fool you. For a fee of $150.00, Car Bargains will pit dealers against one another until the last one standing agrees to give you the best price. Car Bargains takes about a week to

accomplish this and provides you with a report indicating how much above or below invoice price each dealer will sell or lease you a vehicle. You can cross check your dealer report against the factory invoice sheet which Car Bargains includes for your reference.

Phone: 1.800.475.7283
Web: www.checkbook.org

- **Leasing Software**

LeaseWizard® Lease and Loan Analysis Software
Recommended in Motor Trend Magazine and Automobile Magazine's 1997 Leasing & Buying Guide, this handy Windows application can generate a full analysis of your particular lease or loan and give hints on improving your deal. Includes ALG residual values and MSRP's for virtually all makes and models. LeaseWizard can also compare leasing to buying, give you a list of

essential questions to ask the dealer, uncover hidden capital costs and predict how expensive a vehicle you can afford to lease or buy. Available by credit card at: 1-800-838-8778 and downloadable online at: **www.residualvalue.com. Suggested Retail Price:** $29.95. **Street Price:** should be around $19.95

Automotive Lease Guide—Residual Value Software
ALG, the definitive residual value source, makes a little software program which will allow you to search for residual values on any make or model. It's pretty handy and can be updated as ALG updates their numbers. It is available by calling ALG at 805.563.0777.

• **Internet Sources**

The following is a list of Internet sources listed in no particular order. I found over 200 sites doing a search with the words "auto" and "leasing." Here is a smattering (listed alphabetically). Only a few of the sites were particularly impressive, but I will leave it up to you to decide. Under each site is a brief description of the service that seemed to stand out. The information and pricing was accurate as of the date of this book was submitted for printing.

Advanced Auto Leasing
URL: http://www.wanet.net/~aleasing/
SERVICE: Download printed general info

AutoBuy
URL: http://www.webcom.com/~autobuy/
SERVICE: 900-number info service $5.95

Auto Lease Store
URL: http://www.residualvalue.com
SERVICE: Free ALG residual values on new models. Should have editorial advice and bank rates by mid-1997.

AutoSite

URL: http://www.autosite.com

SERVICE: Mainly auto repair and troubleshooting reports. Also offers recall information and other tidbits. For $9.95 you get a month of unlimited access to pricing information and beefed-up reports.

AutoVantage

URL: http://www.autovantage.com/

SERVICE: Automobile locator service.

ALG Residual Values

URL: http://www.residualvalue.com/

SERVICE: Residual value data; good tips on leasing. Free searches (limited to 5 per month).

Car Secrets

URL: http://www.igs.net/carsecrets/

SERVICE: $27.00 for a book with 300 "secrets revealed" For the price, the secrets had better be good!

CarBargains
URL: http://www.checkbook.org/carbarg.htm
SERVICE: Shopping service - $150.00 (see above description)

CarPoint
URL: http://carpoint.msn.com/
SERVICE: This is Microsoft's foray into Internet automobile madness. Worth a look!

DealerNet
URL: http://www.dealernet.com/
SERVICE: Watch out! The graphics on this site are as slick as . . . well, you know. The site will help you find local dealerships with your vehicle of choice and along the way, get you into General Electric's consumer finance database!

Edmund's
URL: http://www.edmunds.com/
SERVICE: Pricing information. Although this site is graphically challenged, the site is speedy

and provides good information that is available at other similar sites.

Fleet Management Resources, Inc.
URL: http://www.fleet-mgt.com/
SERVICE: $24.95 for lease vs. buy comparison

Kelley Blue Book
URL: http://www.kbb.com/
SERVICE: This site is a no-nonsense, up-to-date pricing source.

Motor Trend
URL: http://www.motortrend.com/
SERVICE: The name speaks for itself! This is an excellent site to obtain information and other resources for leasing, purchasing and other areas of automobile interest.

Vehicle Zone
URL:http://www.vehiclezone.com/
SERVICE: Similar to Auto-By-Tel (Great web site!)

Regulation M—Full Text
Appendix B

The following is the full text of Regulation M, the regulations to the Consumer Leasing Act.[18]

Contents of Regulation

---

[18]For those interested, on September 28, 1996, the House passed the Economic Growth and Regulatory Paperwork Reduction Act of 1996, which included certain provisions mandating the amendment of the Consumer Leasing Act. This bill gave legislative support to the Federal Reserve Board's actions and also mandated certain broad parameters of the Regulation.

Regulation Text

§ 213.1 Authority, scope, purpose, and enforcement.

(a) **Authority.** The regulation in this part, known as Regulation M, is issued by the Board of Governors of the Federal Reserve System to implement the consumer leasing provisions of the Truth in Lending Act, which is Title I of the Consumer Credit Protection Act, as amended (15 U.S.C. 1601 et seq.).

(b) **Scope and purpose.** This part applies to all persons that are lessors of personal property under consumer leases as those terms are defined in § 213.2(e)(1) and (h). The purpose of this part is:

(1) To ensure that lessees of personal property receive meaningful disclosures that enable them to compare lease terms with other leases and, where appropriate, with credit transactions.

(2) To limit the amount of balloon payments in consumer lease transactions; and

(3) To provide for the accurate disclosure of lease terms in advertising.

(c) **Enforcement and liability.** Section 108 of the act contains the administrative enforcement provisions. Sections 112, 130, 131, and 185 of the act contain the liability provisions for failing to comply with the requirements of the act and this part.

§ 213.2 Definitions.

For the purposes of this part the following definitions apply:

(a) *Act* means the Truth in Lending Act (15 U.S.C. 1601 et seq.) and the Consumer Leasing Act is chapter 5.

(b) *Advertisement* means a commercial message in any medium that directly or indirectly promotes a consumer lease transaction.

(c) *Board* refers to the Board of Governors of the Federal Reserve System.

(d) *Closed-end lease* means a consumer lease other than an open-end lease as defined in this section.

(e)　(1) *Consumer lease* means a contract in the form of a bailment or lease for the use of personal property by a natural person primarily for personal, family, or household purposes, for a period exceeding four months and for a total contractual obligation not exceeding $25,000, whether or not the lessee has the option to purchase or otherwise become the owner of the property at the expiration of the lease. Unless the context indicates otherwise, in this part "lease" means "consumer lease."

(2) The term does not include a lease that meets the definition of a credit sale in Regulation Z (12 CFR 226.2(a)). It also does not include a lease for agricultural, business, or commercial purposes or a lease made to an organization.

(3) This part does not apply to a lease transaction of personal property which is incident to the lease of real property and which provides that:

> (i) the lessee has no liability for the value of the personal property at the end of the lease term except for abnormal wear and tear, and

> (ii) the lessee has no option to purchase the leased property.

(f) ***Gross capitalized cost*** means the amount agreed upon by the lessor and the lessee as the value of the leased property and any items that are capitalized or amortized during the lease term, including but not limited to taxes, insurance, service agreements, and any outstanding balance from a prior loan or lease. Capitalized cost reduction means the total amount of any rebate, cash payment, net trade-in allowance, and noncash credit that reduces the gross capitalized cost. The adjusted capitalized cost equals the gross capitalized cost less the capitalized cost reduction, and is the amount used by the lessor in calculating the base periodic payment.

(g) ***Lessee*** means a natural person who enters into or is offered a consumer lease.

(h) ***Lessor*** means a person who regularly leases, offers to lease, or arranges for the lease of personal property under a consumer lease. A person who has leased, offered, or arranged to lease personal property more than five times in the preceding calendar year or more than five times in the current calendar year is subject to the act and this part.

(i) *Open-end lease* means a consumer lease in which the lessee's liability at the end of the lease term is based on the difference between the residual value of the leased property and its realized value.

(j) *Organization* means a corporation, trust, estate, partnership, cooperative, association, or government entity or instrumentality.

(k) *Person* means a natural person or an organization.

(l) *Personal property* means any property that is not real property under the law of the state where the property is located at the time it is offered or made available for lease.

(m) *Realized value* means:

> (1) The price received by the lessor for the leased property at disposition;

(2) The highest offer for disposition of the leased property; or

(3) The fair market value of the leased property at the end of the lease term.

(n) *Residual value* means the value of the leased property at the end of the lease term, as estimated or assigned at consummation by the lessor, used in calculating the base periodic payment.

(o) *Security interest and security* mean any interest in property that secures the payment or performance of an obligation.

(p) *State* means any state, the District of Columbia, the Commonwealth of Puerto Rico, and any territory or possession of the United States.

§ 213.3 General disclosure requirements.

(a) **General requirements.** A lessor shall make the disclosures required by § 213.4, as applicable. The disclosures shall be made clearly and conspicuously in writing in a form the consumer may keep, in accordance with this section.

(1) **Form of disclosures.** The disclosures required by § 213.4 shall be given to the lessee together in a dated statement that identifies the lessor and the lessee; the disclosures may be made either in a separate statement that identifies the consumer lease transaction or in the contract or other document evidencing the lease. Alternatively, the disclosures required to be segregated from other information under paragraph (a)(2) of this section may be provided in a separate dated statement that identifies the lease, and the other required disclosures may be provided in the lease contract or other document evidencing the lease. In a lease of multiple items, the property description required by § 213.4(a) may be given in a separate statement that is incorporated by reference in the disclosure statement required by this paragraph.

(2) **Segregation of certain disclosures.** The following disclosures shall be segregated from other information and shall contain only directly related information: §§ 213.4(b) through (f), (g)(2), (h)(3), (i)(1), (j), and (m)(1). The headings, content, and format for the disclosures referred to in this paragraph shall be provided in a manner substantially similar to the applicable model form in appendix A of this part.

(3) **Timing of disclosures.** A lessor shall provide the disclosures to the lessee prior to the consummation of a consumer lease.

(4) **Language of disclosures.** The disclosures required by § 213.4 may be made in a language other than English provided that they are made available in English upon the lessee's request.

(b) **Additional information; nonsegregated disclosures.** Additional information may be provided with any disclosure not listed in paragraph (a)(2) of this section, but it shall not be stated, used, or placed so as to mislead or confuse the lessee or contradict, obscure, or detract attention from any disclosure required by this part.

(c) **Multiple lessors or lessees.** When a transaction involves more than one lessor, the disclosures required by this part may be made by one lessor on behalf of all the lessors. When a lease involves more than one lessee, the lessor may provide the disclosures to any lessee who is primarily liable on the lease.

(d) **Use of estimates.** If an amount or other item needed to comply with a required disclosure is unknown or unavailable after reasonable efforts have been made to ascertain the information, the lessor may use a reasonable estimate that is based on the best information available to the lessor, is clearly identified as an estimate, and is not used to circumvent or evade any disclosures required by this part.

(e) **Effect of subsequent occurrence.** If a required

disclosure becomes inaccurate because of an event occurring after consummation, the inaccuracy is not a violation of this part. (f) Minor variations. A lessor may disregard the effects of the following in making disclosures:

(1) That payments must be collected in whole cents;

(2) That dates of scheduled payments may be different because a scheduled date is not a business day;

(3) That months have different numbers of days; and

(4) That February 29 occurs in a leap year.

§ 213.4 Content of disclosures.

For any consumer lease subject to this part, the lessor shall disclose the following information, as applicable:

(a) **Description of property.** A brief description of the leased property sufficient to identify the property to the lessee and lessor.

(b) **Amount due at lease signing.** The total amount to be paid prior to or at consummation, using the term "amount due at lease signing." The lessor shall itemize each component by type and amount, including any refundable security deposit, advance monthly or other periodic payment, and capitalized cost reduction; and in motor-vehicle leases, shall itemize how the amount due will be paid, by type and amount, including any net trade-in allowance, rebates, noncash credits, and cash payments in a format substantially similar to the model forms in appendix A of this part.

(c) **Payment schedule and total amount of periodic payments.** The number, amount, and due dates or periods of payments scheduled under the lease, and the total amount of the periodic payments.

(d) **Other charges.** The total amount of other charges payable to the lessor, itemized by type and amount, that are not included in the periodic payments. Such charges include the amount of any liability the lease imposes upon the lessee at the end of the lease term; the potential difference between the residual and realized values referred to in paragraph (k) of this section is excluded.

(e) **Total of payments.** The total of payments, with a description such as "the amount you will have paid by the end of the lease." This amount is the sum of the amount due at lease signing (less any refundable amounts), the total amount of periodic payments (less any portion of the periodic payment paid at lease signing), and other charges under paragraphs (b), (c), and (d) of this section. In an open-end lease, a description such as "you will owe an additional amount if the actual value of the vehicle is less than the residual value" shall accompany the disclosure.

(f) **Payment calculation.** In a motor-vehicle lease, a mathematical progression of how the scheduled periodic payment is derived, in a format substantially similar to the applicable model form in appendix A of this part, which shall contain the following:

(1) ***Gross capitalized cost.*** The gross capitalized cost, including a disclosure of the agreed upon value of the vehicle, a description such as "the agreed upon value of the vehicle [state the amount] and any items you pay for over the lease term (such as service contracts, insurance, and any outstanding prior loan or lease balance)," and a statement of the lessee's option to receive a separate written itemization of the gross capitalized cost. If requested by the lessee, the itemization shall be provided before consummation.

(2) ***Capitalized cost reduction.*** The capitalized cost reduction, with a description such as "the amount of any net trade-in allowance, rebate, noncash credit, or cash you pay that reduces the gross capitalized cost."

(3) *Adjusted capitalized cost.* The adjusted capitalized cost, with a description such as "the amount used in calculating your base [periodic] payment."

(4) *Residual value.* The residual value, with a description such as "the value of the vehicle at the end of the lease used in calculating your base [periodic] payment."

(5) *Depreciation and any amortized amounts.* The depreciation and any amortized amounts, which is the difference between the adjusted capitalized cost and the residual value, with a description such as "the amount charged for the vehicle's decline in value through normal use and for any other items paid over the lease term."

(6) *Rent charge.* The rent charge, with a description such as "the amount charged in addition to the depreciation and any amortized amounts." This amount is the difference

between the total of the base periodic payments over the lease term minus the depreciation and any amortized amounts.

(7) *Total of base periodic payments.* The total of base periodic payments with a description such as "depreciation and any amortized amounts plus the rent charge."

(8) *Lease term.* The lease term with a description such as "the number of [periods of repayment] in your lease."

(9) *Base periodic payment.* The total of the base periodic payments divided by the number of payment periods in the lease.

(10) *Itemization of other charges.* An itemization of any other charges that are part of the periodic payment.

(11) ***Total periodic payment.*** The sum of the base periodic payment and any other charges that are part of the periodic payment.

(g) **Early termination.**

(1) *Conditions and disclosure of charges.* A statement of the conditions under which the lessee or lessor may terminate the lease prior to the end of the lease term; and the amount or a description of the method for determining the amount of any penalty or other charge for early termination, which must be reasonable.

(2) *Early-termination notice.* In a motor-vehicle lease, a notice substantially similar to the following: "Early Termination. You may have to pay a substantial charge if you end this lease early. The charge may be up to several thousand dollars. The actual charge will depend on when the lease is terminated. The earlier you end the lease, the greater this charge is likely to be."

(h) **Maintenance responsibilities.**

(1) *Statement of responsibilities.* A statement specifying whether the lessor or the lessee is responsible for maintaining or servicing the leased property, together with a brief description of the responsibility;

(2) *Wear and use standard.* A statement of the lessor's standards for wear and use (if any), which must be reasonable; and

(3) *Notice of wear and use standard.* In a motor- vehicle lease, a notice regarding wear and use substantially similar to the following: "Excessive Wear and Use. You may be charged for excessive wear based on our standards for normal use." The notice shall also specify the amount or method for determining any charge for excess mileage.

(i) **Purchase option.** A statement of whether or not the lessee has the option to purchase the leased property, and:

(1) *End of lease term.* If at the end of the lease term, the purchase price; and

(2) *During lease term.* If prior to the end of the lease term, the purchase price or the method for determining the price and when the lessee may exercise this option.

(j) **Statement referencing nonsegregated disclosures.** A statement that the lessee should refer to the lease documents for additional information on early termination, purchase options and maintenance responsibilities, warranties, late and default charges, insurance, and any security interests, if applicable.

(k) **Liability between residual and realized values.** A statement of the lessee's liability, if any, at early termination or at the end of the lease term for the difference between the residual value of the leased property and its realized value.

(l) **Right of appraisal.** If the lessee's liability at early termination or at the end of the lease term is based on

170

the realized value of the leased property, a statement that the lessee may obtain, at the lessee's expense, a professional appraisal by an independent third party (agreed to by the lessee and the lessor) of the value that could be realized at sale of the leased property. The appraisal shall be final and binding on the parties.

(m) **Liability at end of lease term based on residual value.** If the lessee is liable at the end of the lease term for the difference between the residual value of the leased property and its realized value:

(1) *Rent and other charges.* The rent and other charges, paid by the lessee and required by the lessor as an incident to the lease transaction, with a description such as "the total amount of rent and other charges imposed in connection with your lease [state the amount]."

(2) *Excess liability.* A statement about a rebuttable presumption that, at the end of the lease term, the residual value of the leased property is unreasonable and not in good faith

to the extent that the residual value exceeds the realized value by more than three times the base monthly payment (or more than three times the average payment allocable to a monthly period, if the lease calls for periodic payments other than monthly); and that the lessor cannot collect the excess amount unless the lessor brings a successful court action and pays the lessee's reasonable attorney's fees, or unless the excess of the residual value over the realized value is due to unreasonable or excessive wear or use of the leased property (in which case the rebuttable presumption does not apply).

(3) *Mutually agreeable final adjustment.* A statement that the lessee and lessor are permitted, after termination of the lease, to make any mutually agreeable final adjustment regarding excess liability.

(n) **Fees and taxes.** The total dollar amount for all official and license fees, registration, title, or taxes required to be paid to the lessor in connection with the lease.

(o) **Insurance.** A brief identification of insurance in connection with the lease including:

(1) *Voluntary insurance.* If the insurance is provided by or paid through the lessor, the types and amounts of coverage and the cost to the lessee; or

(2) *Required insurance.* If the lessee must obtain the insurance, the types and amounts of coverage required of the lessee.

(p) **Warranties or guarantees.** A statement identifying all express warranties and guarantees from the manufacturer or lessor with respect to the leased property that apply to the lessee.

(q) **Penalties and other charges for delinquency.** The amount or the method of determining the amount of any penalty or other charge for delinquency, default, or late payments, which must be reasonable.

(r) **Security interest.** A description of any security interest, other than a security deposit disclosed under paragraph (b) of this section, held or to be retained by the lessor; and a clear identification of the property to which the security interest relates.

(s) **Limitations on rate information.** If a lessor provides a percentage rate in an advertisement or in documents evidencing the lease transaction, a notice stating that "this percentage may not measure the overall cost of financing this lease" shall accompany the rate disclosure. The lessor shall not use the term "annual percentage rate," "annual lease rate," or any equivalent term.

§ 213.5 Renegotiations, extensions, and assumptions.

(a) **Renegotiation.** A renegotiation occurs when a consumer lease subject to this part is satisfied and replaced by a new lease undertaken by the same consumer. A renegotiation requires new disclosures, except as provided in paragraph (d) of this section.

(b) **Extension.** An extension is a continuation, agreed to by the lessor and the lessee, of an existing consumer lease beyond the originally scheduled end of the lease term, except when the continuation is the result of a renegotiation. An extension that exceeds six months requires new disclosures, except as provided in paragraph (d) of this section.

(c) **Assumption.** New disclosures are not required when a consumer lease is assumed by another person, whether or not the lessor charges an assumption fee.

(d) **Exceptions.** New disclosures are not required for the following, even if they meet the definition of a renegotiation or an extension:

(1) A reduction in the lease charge;

(2) The deferment of one or more payments, whether or not a fee is charged;

(3) The extension of a lease for not more than six months on a month-to-month basis or otherwise;

(4) A substitution of leased property with property that has a substantially equivalent or greater economic value, provided no other lease terms are changed;

(5) The addition, deletion, or substitution of leased property in a multiple-item lease, provided the average periodic payment does not change by more than 25 percent; or

(6) An agreement resulting from a court proceeding.

§ 213.6 [Reserved]

§ 213.7 Advertising.

(a) **General rule.** An advertisement for a consumer lease may state that a specific lease of property at specific amounts or terms is available only if the lessor usually and customarily leases or will lease the property at those amounts or terms.

(b) **Clear and conspicuous standard.** Disclosures required by this section shall be made clearly and conspicuously.

(1) *Amount due at lease signing.* Except for the statement of a periodic payment, any affirmative or negative reference to a charge that is a part of the total amount due at lease signing under § 213.7(d)(2)(ii), such as the amount of any capitalized cost reduction (or no capitalized cost reduction is required), shall not be more prominent than the disclosure of the total amount due at lease signing.

(2) *Advertisement of a lease rate.* If a lessor provides a percentage rate in an advertisement, the rate shall not be more prominent than any of the disclosures in § 213.4, with the exception of the notice in § 213.4(s) required to accompany

177

the rate; and the lessor shall not use the term "annual percentage rate," "annual lease rate," or equivalent term.

(c) **Catalogs and multipage advertisements.** A catalog or other multipage advertisement that provides a table or schedule of the required disclosures shall be considered a single advertisement if, for lease terms that appear without all the required disclosures, the advertisement refers to the page or pages on which the table or schedule appears.

(d) **Advertisement of terms that require additional disclosure.**

(1) *Triggering terms.* An advertisement that states any of the following items shall contain the disclosures required by paragraph (d)(2), except as provided in paragraphs (e) and (f) of this section:

(i) The amount of any payment;

(ii) The number of required payments; or

(iii) A statement of any capitalized cost reduction or other payment required prior to or at consummation, or that no payment is required.

(2) *Additional terms.* An advertisement stating any item listed in paragraph (d)(1) of this section shall also state the following items:

(i) That the transaction advertised is a lease;

(ii) The total amount due at lease signing, or that no payment is required;

(iii) The number, amounts, due dates or periods of scheduled payments, and total of such payments under the lease;

(iv) A statement of whether or not the lessee has the option to purchase the leased property, and where the lessee has the option to purchase at the end of the lease term, the purchase-option price. The method of determining the purchase-option price may be substituted in disclosing the lessee's option to purchase the leased property prior to the end of the lease term;

(v) A statement of the amount, or the method for determining the amount, of the lessee's liability (if any) at the end of the lease term; and

(vi) A statement of the lessee's liability (if any) for the difference between the residual value of the leased property and its realized value at the end of the lease term.

(e) **Alternative disclosures—merchandise tags.** A merchandise tag stating any item listed in paragraph (d)(1) may comply with paragraph (d)(2) by referring to a sign or display prominently posted in the lessor's place of business that contains a table or schedule of the required disclosures.

(f) **Alternative disclosures—television or radio advertisements.**

(1) Toll-free number or print advertisement. An advertisement made through television or radio stating any item listed in paragraph (d)(1) complies with paragraph (d)(2) if the advertisement states the items listed in paragraphs (d)(2)(i)-(iii) of this section, and:

(i) Lists a toll-free telephone number along with a reference that such number may be used by consumers to obtain the information required by paragraph (d)(2) of this section; or

(ii) Directs the consumer to a written advertisement in a publication of general circulation in the community served by the media station, including the name and the date of the publication, with a statement that information required by paragraph (d)(2) of this section is

181

included in the advertisement. The written advertisement shall be published beginning at least three days before and ending at least ten days after the broadcast.

(2) Establishment of toll-free number. (i) The toll-free telephone number shall be available for no fewer than ten days, beginning on the date of the broadcast. (ii) The lessor shall provide the information required by paragraph (d)(2) of this section orally, or in writing upon request.

§ 213.8 Record Retention.

A lessor shall retain evidence of compliance with the requirements imposed by this part, other than the advertising requirements under § 213.7, for a period of not less than two years after the date the disclosures are required to be made or an action is required to be taken.

§ 213.9 Relation to state laws.

(a) **Inconsistent state law.** A state law that is inconsistent with the requirements of the act and this part is preempted to the extent of the inconsistency. If a lessor cannot comply with a state law without violating a provision of this part, the state law is inconsistent within the meaning of section 186(a) of the act and is preempted, unless the state law gives greater protection and benefit to the consumer. A state, through an official having primary enforcement or interpretative responsibilities for the state consumer leasing law, may apply to the Board for a preemption determination.

(b) **Exemptions.**

(1) *Application.* A state may apply to the Board for an exemption from the requirements of the act and this part for any class of lease transactions within the state. The Board will grant such an exemption if the Board determines that:

(i) The class of leasing transactions is subject to state law requirements substantially similar to the act and this part or that lessees are afforded greater protection under state law; and

(ii) There is adequate provision for state enforcement.

(2) *Enforcement and liability.* After an exemption has been granted, the requirements of the applicable state law (except for additional requirements not imposed by federal law) will constitute the requirements of the act and this part. No exemption will extend to the civil liability provisions of sections 130, 131, and 185 of the act.

Appendix A-1 Model Open-End or Finance Vehicle Lease Disclosures

Federal Consumer Leasing Act Disclosures

Date _____

Lessor(s) _____   Lessee(s) _____

Amount Due at Lease Signing	Monthly Payments	Other Charges (not part of your monthly payment)	Total of Payments (The amount you will have paid by the end of the lease)
(itemized below)* $ _____	Your first monthly payment of $ _____ is due on _____, followed by _____ payments of $ _____ due on the _____ of each month. The total of your monthly payments is $ _____.	Disposition fee (if you do not purchase the vehicle) $ _____ [Annual tax] _____ Total $ _____	$ _____ You will owe an additional amount if the actual value of the vehicle is less than the residual value.

* Itemization of Amount Due at Lease Signing

Amount Due At Lease Signing:		How the Amount Due at Lease Signing will be paid:	
Capitalized cost reduction	$ _____	Net trade-in allowance	$ _____
First monthly payment	_____	Rebates and noncash credits	_____
Refundable security deposit	_____	Amount to be paid in cash	_____
Title fees	_____		
Registration fees	_____		
Total	$ _____	Total	$ _____

Your monthly payment is determined as shown below:

Gross capitalized cost. The agreed upon value of the vehicle ($ _____) and any items you pay over the lease term (such as service contracts, insurance, and any outstanding prior loan or lease balance) .... $ _____

If you want an itemization of this amount, please check this box. ☐

Capitalized cost reduction. The amount of any net trade-in allowance, rebate, noncash credit, or cash you pay
that reduces the gross capitalized cost .... − _____
Adjusted capitalized cost. The amount used in calculating your base monthly payment .... = _____
Residual value. The value of the vehicle at the end of the lease used in calculating your base monthly payment .... − _____
Depreciation and any amortized amounts. The amount charged for the vehicle's decline in value
through normal use and for other items paid over the lease term .... = _____
Rent charge. The amount charged in addition to the depreciation and any amortized amounts .... + _____
Total of base monthly payments. The depreciation and any amortized amounts plus the rent charge .... = _____
Lease term. The number of months in your lease .... ÷ _____
Base monthly payment .... = _____
Monthly sales/use tax .... + _____
_____ + _____
Total monthly payment .... = $ _____

Rent and other charges. The total amount of rent and other charges imposed in connection with your lease $ _____ .

Early Termination. You may have to pay a substantial charge if you end this lease early. The charge may be up to several thousand dollars. The actual charge will depend on when the lease is terminated. The earlier you end the lease, the greater this charge is likely to be.

Excessive Wear and Use. You may be charged for excessive wear based on our standards for normal use [and for mileage in excess of _____ miles per year at the rate of _____ per mile].

Purchase Option at End of Lease Term. [You have an option to purchase the vehicle at the end of the lease term for $ _____ [and a purchase option fee of $ _____].] [You do not have an option to purchase the vehicle at the end of the lease term.]

Other Important Terms. See your lease documents for additional information on early termination, purchase options and maintenance responsibilities, warranties, late and default charges, insurance, and any security interest, if applicable.

[The following provisions are the nonsegregated disclosures required under Regulation M.]

Official Fees and Taxes. The total amount you will pay for official and license fees, registration, title, and taxes over the term of your lease, whether included with your monthly payments or assessed otherwise: $ _____ .

Insurance. The following types and amounts of insurance will be acquired in connection with this lease:

_____ .

_____ We (lessor) will provide the insurance coverage quoted above for a total premium cost of $ _____ .

_____ You (lessee) agree to provide insurance coverage in the amount and types indicated above.

End of Term Liability. (a) The residual value ($ _____) of the vehicle is based on a reasonable, good faith estimate of the value of the vehicle at the end of the lease term. If the actual value of the vehicle at that time is greater than the residual value, you will have no further liability under this lease, except for other charges already incurred [and are entitled to a credit or refund of any surplus.] If the actual value of the vehicle is less than the residual value, you will be liable for any difference up to $ _____ (3 times the monthly payment). For any difference in excess of that amount, you will be liable only if:
1. Excessive use or damage [as described in paragraph ____] [representing more than normal wear and use] resulted in an unusually low value at the end of the term.
2. The matter is not otherwise resolved and we win a lawsuit against you seeking a higher payment.
3. You voluntarily agree with us after the end of the lease term to make a higher payment.
Should we bring a lawsuit against you, we must prove that our original estimate of the value of the leased property at the end of the lease term was reasonable and was made in good faith. For example, we might prove that the actual was less than the original estimated value, although the original estimate was reasonable, because of an unanticipated decline in value for that type of vehicle. We must also pay your attorney's fees.
(b) If you disagree with the value we assign to the vehicle, you may obtain, at your own expense, from an independent third party agreeable to both of us, a professional appraisal of the _____ value of the leased vehicle which could be realized at sale. The appraised value shall then be used as the actual value.

Standards for Wear and Use. The following standards are applicable for determining unreasonable or excess wear and use of the leased vehicle:

_____ .

Maintenance.
[You are responsible for the following maintenance and servicing of the leased vehicle:

_____].

[We are responsible for the following maintenance and servicing of the leased vehicle:

_____].

Warranties. The leased vehicle is subject to the following express warranties:

_____

Early Termination and Default. (a) You may terminate this lease before the end of the lease term under the following conditions:

_____ .

The charge for such early termination is:

_____

(b) We may terminate this lease before the end of the lease term under the following conditions:

_____

Upon such termination we shall be entitled to the following charge(s) for:

_____ .

(c) To the extent these charges take into account the value of the vehicle at termination, if you disagree with the value we assign to the vehicle, you may obtain, at your own expense, from an independent third party agreeable to both of us, a professional appraisal of the _____ value of the leased vehicle which could be realized at sale. The appraised value shall then be used as the actual value.

Security Interest. We reserve a security interest of the following type in the property listed below to secure performance of your obligations under this lease:

_____ .

Late Payments. The charge for late payments is: _____

Option to Purchase Leased Property Prior to the End of the Lease. [You have an option to purchase the leased vehicle prior to the end of the term. The price will be [$ _____ /[the method of determining the price].] [You do not have an option to purchase the leased vehicle.]

Appendix A-2 Model Closed-End or Net Vehicle Lease Disclosures

Federal Consumer Leasing Act Disclosures

Date _____

Lessor(s) _____   Lessee(s) _____

Amount Due at Lease Signing	Monthly Payments	Other Charges (not part of your monthly payment)	Total of Payments (The amount you will have paid by the end of the lease)
(Itemized below)*	Your first monthly payment of $ _____ is due on _____, followed by _____ payments of $ _____ due on the _____ of each month. The total of your monthly payments is $ _____.	Disposition fee (if you do not purchase the vehicle) $ _____ [Annual tax] _____ _____ Total $ _____	$ _____
$ _____			

* Itemization of Amount Due at Lease Signing

Amount Due At Lease Signing:		How the Amount Due at Lease Signing will be paid:	
Capitalized cost reduction	$ _____	Net trade-in allowance	$ _____
First monthly payment	_____	Rebates and noncash credits	_____
Refundable security deposit	_____	Amount to be paid in cash	_____
Title fees	_____		
Registration fees	_____		
Total	$ _____	Total	$ _____

Your monthly payment is determined as shown below:

Gross capitalized cost. The agreed upon value of the vehicle ($ _____) and any items you pay over the lease term (such as service contracts, insurance, and any outstanding prior loan or lease balance) .... $ _____

If you want an itemization of this amount, please check this box. ☐

Capitalized cost reduction. The amount of any net trade-in allowance, rebate, noncash credit, or cash you pay that reduces the gross capitalized cost .... − _____

Adjusted capitalized cost. The amount used in calculating your base monthly payment .... = _____

Residual value. The value of the vehicle at the end of the lease used in calculating your base monthly payment .... − _____

Depreciation and any amortized amounts. The amount charged for the vehicle's decline in value through normal use and for other items paid over the lease term .... = _____

Rent charge. The amount charged in addition to the depreciation and any amortized amounts .... + _____

Total of base monthly payments. The depreciation and any amortized amounts plus the rent charge .... = _____

Lease term. The number of months in your lease .... ÷ _____

Base monthly payment. .... = _____

Monthly sales/use tax .... + _____

_____ .... + _____

Total monthly payment .... = $ _____

Early Termination. You may have to pay a substantial charge if you end this lease early. <u>The charge may be up to several thousand dollars.</u> The actual charge will depend on when the lease is terminated. The earlier you end the lease, the greater this charge is likely to be.

Excessive Wear and Use. You may be charged for excessive wear based on our standards for normal use [and for mileage in excess of _____ miles per year at the rate of _____ per mile].

Purchase Option at End of Lease Term. [You have an option to purchase the vehicle at the end of the lease term for $ _____ [and a purchase option fee of $ _____].] [You do not have an option to purchase the vehicle at the end of the lease term.]

Other Important Terms. See your lease documents for additional information on early termination, purchase options and maintenance responsibilities, warranties, late and default charges, insurance, and any security interest, if applicable.

[The following provisions are the nonsegregated disclosures required under Regulation M.]

Official Fees and Taxes. The total amount you will pay for official and license fees, registration, title, and taxes over the term of your lease, whether included with your monthly payments or assessed otherwise: $ _____ .

Insurance. The following types and amounts of insurance will be acquired in connection with this lease:

_____ .

_____ We (lessor) will provide the insurance coverage quoted above for a total premium cost of $ _____ .

_____ You (lessee) agree to provide insurance coverage in the amount and types indicated above.

Standards for Wear and Use. The following standards are applicable for determining unreasonable or excess wear and use of the leased vehicle:

_____ .

Maintenance.
[You are responsible for the following maintenance and servicing of the leased vehicle:

_____].

[We are responsible for the following maintenance and servicing of the leased vehicle:

_____].

Warranties. The leased vehicle is subject to the following express warranties:

_____ .

Early Termination and Default. (a) You may terminate this lease before the end of the lease term under the following conditions:

_____ .

The charge for such early termination is:

_____ .

(b) We may terminate this lease before the end of the lease term under the following conditions:

_____ .

Upon such termination we shall be entitled to the following charge(s) for:

_____ .

(c) To the extent these charges take into account the value of the vehicle at termination, if you disagree with the value we assign to the vehicle, you may obtain, at your own expense, from an independent third party agreeable to both of us, a professional appraisal of the _____ value of the leased vehicle which could be realized at sale. The appraised value shall then be used as the actual value.

Security Interest. We reserve a security interest of the following type in the property listed below to secure performance of your obligations under this lease:

_____ .

Late Payments. The charge for late payments is: _____ .

Option to Purchase Leased Property Prior to the End of the Lease. [You have an option to purchase the leased vehicle prior to the end of the term. The price will be [$ _____ /the method of determining the price].] [You do not have an option to purchase the leased vehicle.]

1. **Vehicle Information**
   a. Year/Make/Model _____
   b. Options _____

2. **Purchase Price (Capitalized Cost)**
   a. MSRP (Sticker Price) _____
   b. Dealer Discount/Rebates/ _____
      Other Dealer Reductions <_____>
   c. Dealer's "Best" Price _____
   d. Your Cap Cost Reductions _____
      i.   Trade in allowance <_____>
      ii. Down Payment <_____>
   e. Fees "Rolled" Into Lease _____
      i   Acquisition Fee _____
      ii   Other Fees _____
   f. Luxury Tax Amount _____
   g. ADJ. CAP COST _____

3. **Facts Needed to Analyze Monthly Payment**
   a. Quoted Monthly Payment _____
   b. Residual Value _____
   c. Ann. Rate or Money Factor _____
   d. If no rate, Lease Charge _____
   e. Sales/Use Tax Rate _____
   f. Method of Taxation _____

4. **Other Important Information**
   a. Mileage Cap _____
   b. Excess Mileage Fee _____
   c. Cost to "buy" extra miles _____
   d. Disposition Fee _____
   e. Title and Registration Fees _____
   f. Other Fees (not in payment) _____
   g. Security Deposit _____

Ford Money Factor

F ord Motor Credit uses a money factor that does not, on the surface, appear to be "typical." Rather, they give arbitrary whole numbers (like 4 or 7) which correspond to FMC's internal rates. Since these numbers are of no use to you, you can always ask for the monthly interest payment (lease charge) or the total interest charge to verify the annualized interest rate. Or, if you insist on knowing the true money factor, ask the dealer to give you Ford's corresponding "ACQ" and "LEV" fractions. If Ford has not changed their system, you should be able to derive a money factor in a form useful for analysis by doing the following:

1.   Multiply the ACQ x LEV

2.   Take the result and multiply it by 2

That should give you a "typical" money factor suitable for plugging into the formulae described in this book. Remember, finance companies are usually a step ahead when it comes to devising new ways of expressing money factors. Hopefully, you won't have to go through these mathematical manipulations because the dealer will favor you with an approximate annual rate, a monthly lease charge or a total lease charge. Good luck!

Index